BONSA

Trident maple
Acer buergerianum
rock planting—
Ishitsuki
height 80cm
age about 65 years

BONSAI
The Complete Guide to
Art and Technique

Paul Lesniewicz

Translated by Susan Simpson

CASSELL

Cassell Publishers Limited
Wellington House
125 Strand
London WC2R 0BB

First published in Great Britain 1984

Reprinted 1985, 1986 (three times), 1987 (twice),
1988, 1990, 1992
First paperback edition 1997
Reprinted 1998

Title of the original German edition
Bonsai Miniaturbäume published by BLV Verlag mbH Munich

British Library Cataloguing in Publication Data
A catalogue record for this book is available from the British Library

ISBN 0-304-34943-7

Distributed in the United States by Sterling Publishing Co. Inc.
387 Park Avenue South, New York, N.Y. 10016-8810

Typeset by August Filmsetting, Haydock, St.Helens
Printed in Slovenia by DELO - Tiskarna d.d.
by arrangement with Korotan - Ljubljana, 1998

The author invites readers visiting Heidelberg to inspect his magnifi-
cent collection of bonsai at the Bonsai Museum and Bonsai Centrum,
open weekdays 10.00 to 18.00 and weekends 10.00 to 16.00
at Mannheimer Strasse 401; telephone (0 6221) 8491-0,
fax (0 6221) 849130.

Front jacket *Acer palmatum dissectum*
Moyogi, height 45cm, age about 40 years, in spring

A famous Japanese story tells of an impoverished Samurai who, on a bitterly cold winter's night in 1383, sacrificed his last three, much loved bonsai to the fire to provide some heating for his honoured visitor, a shogun. The wood-block here shows the trees just as they are being chopped down.

Acknowledgements

The publishers of the English language edition and the translator would like to acknowledge the assistance given by Bill Horan of the British Bonsai Association in preparing the English edition of this book.

The author would like to take this opportunity to thank Koichi Itakura, bonsai master of Tokyo, Japan, for his help and collaboration in this project; also the following sources for the use of their excellent photographs:

Kindai-Bonsai, Japan
Photos on pages 4, 16, 18, 19, 20, 21, 22, 23, 54, 55, 78, 95, 107, 121, 122, 124, 149

Saburo Kato, Japan
Photos on pages 17, 32, 33, 113, 117, 125

Takeyama, Japan
Photos on pages 10, 28, 29, 112, 114, 120, 140

Pin Kewpaisal, Thailand
Photos on pages 159, 160, 173

David Fukumoto, Hawaii
Photos on pages 170, 174

Dr Horace Clay, Hawaii
Photos on pages 7, 12, 13

BASF Ludwigshafen, Landwirtschaftliche Versuchsstation Limburger Hof
Photos on pages 150, 151, 152, 153, 154, 155, 156

Rolf and Gisela Kunitsch, Altheim
Photo on page 145

Hella Wolff-Seybold, Konstanz
Photo on page 99

Hans-Jürgen Fuchs, Stuttgart
Photo on page 167

Studio Orthen, Heidelberg
Photos on pages 50, 56, 73, 79, 104, 105, 108, 109, 118, 139, 143, 147, 148, 165

E. Grames, Cologne
Photos on pages 41, 42, 43, 201

The photos on pages 14, 25, 26, 27, 30, 31, 34, 35, 44, 45, 47, 48, 49, 57, 75, 76, 77, 82, 83, 98, 110, 111, 115, 116, 126, 132, 133, 134, 137, 142, 157, 163, 164, 169, 171, 172, 175 were prepared in the Heidelberg Bonsai Centre by Mr Josef Wiegand.

All the drawings are by Studio C. Rieger, Heidelberg, with the exception of those on pages 190, 191 and 192 which were prepared by K. H. Kindel, Dobel.

Contents

Foreword

Bonsai are living works of art. They cannot be compared with any other artform. A painting or a piece of sculpture is complete once the painter has put down his paintbrush or the sculptor his chisel. A bonsai can never be a finished work of art in this sense because it will always be a living piece of nature, continuing to live and grow.

It is not enough simply to admire the beauty of these miniature trees. The admirer ought to be able to gain from them something much more fundamental: an awareness of the laws of evolution and growth, the realisation that we are all, Man and nature, bound together in these laws.

Paul Lesniewicz, I know, also believes that the bonsai style teaches us this significance. That is why I consider his book an important work, and I wish him every success with it.

John Naka,
President of the California Bonsai Society, Director of Bonsai Clubs International

Mountain maple *Acer palmatum*, raft style—Ikada, height approximately 50cm, age about 35 years

1 WHAT IS A BONSAI? INTRODUCTION AND HISTORY

A bonsai is a tree or shrub grown in a container. Though seldom exceeding 70 cm in height, it makes us believe when we look at it that here is a tree just as it grows in nature. The word 'bonsai' is formed from two words, 'bon' meaning tray or dish and 'sai' meaning tree or plant, so its literal translation is 'tree planted in a dish'. A bonsai is, then, a tree—a miniaturised tree—grown in a dish and resembling in all respects its large counterpart in nature.

The art of bonsai was developed in the Far East where it is considered an expression of the harmony between heaven and earth, Man and nature. Its spiritual foundations lie in the Eastern philosophy of life which strives after harmony between Man and nature—a harmony which becomes apparent when empathy is achieved with the process of all growth and development. There could surely be no more fitting example of this than the cultivation of bonsai.

The lover of bonsai will take time to care for and examine his trees. Through them he experiences anew the rhythm of the seasons, and nurtures within himself the power of creativity as he shapes and miniaturises his little trees. Cultivating a bonsai tree requires much care and attention, but as its reward it brings a tranquillity to the mind, a feeling of being refreshed and of inner composure.

Surely no one can fail to be enchanted by these perfect little trees growing in dishes and resembling in every detail except size trees growing in the wild? A bit of skill is needed to shape and tend them, but anyone who has had luck with other plants will get a great deal of pleasure from his bonsai. The Chinese were the first to plant miniature trees in dishes, and even today bonsai is part of Chinese culture. It has a place in every Chinese community, even outside China itself, in places like Taiwan, Thailand, Hong Kong and Singapore.

Chinese bonsai masters of today still make a distinction between 'pun-sai' and 'pun-ching'. For many the word 'pen-jing' is taken to mean both forms of bonsai. The word 'pun-sai' is made up of the same characters as the Japanese word 'bonsai', and means a tree planted in a container without any landscape, while 'pun-ching' means a tree that is planted in a container or on a tray and landscaped. The art of pun-

In the foreground of this ancient scroll painting are three bonsai— a pine, an apricot and a flowering cherry. They were painted in 1351 by the brothers Takaaki and Takamasa Fujiwara.

ching dates far back to the early period of the Han dynasty, about 206 BC–AD 220, when Chinese landscape artists started to design miniature versions of the already famous artificial rock gardens. According to legend Jiang-feng was endowed with a magic power to conjure up on a dish tiny landscapes complete with rocks, mountains, trees, rivers, houses, people and animals.

At about the same time as the mention of pun-ching, or miniature landscapes with rocks and trees, a form still very popular in China today, we find the first reference to pun-sai during the Ch'in dynasty (221–206 BC): it was Ton Guen-ming; a famous poet and high-ranking official, who, having grown weary of affairs of state, retired to a peaceful country living where he began to cultivate chrysanthemums in pots. This may have been the beginning of pot plants, but it was to lead on to the miniaturisation of trees. Just 200 years later in paintings from the T'ang period we find pines, cypresses, plum trees, and bamboos—all growing in dishes.

Even before the year AD 1000, in the Sung dynasty, there are poems describing pun-sai as well as a wealth of literature on how to form them.

During the period of peace known as the Ch'ing dynasty (AD 1644–1911) both pun-ching and pun-sai became a hobby not only of the aristocracy but of all strata of society in China.

But it was not the Chinese who introduced the art of bonsai to the West; it was the Japanese, first in Paris at the World Fair of 1878, and subsequently in London in 1909.

Buddhist monks probably took bonsai to Japan in the tenth and eleventh centuries. For them they were religious objects, 'verdant stairways leading to Heaven', thus a connection between God and mankind.

During the Yuan dynasty (AD 1280–1368) Japanese government ministers and merchants brought home bonsai as presents from China and we know of Chu Shun-sui, a Chinese official, who, around 1644, fled from the rule of the Manchus to Japan, taking with him his entire collection of bonsai literature. It was his specialist knowledge that contributed decisively to the spread of the art of bonsai in Japan. Around this time Japan was beginning to establish its own form of bonsai cultivation, an art which was at first the preserve of the Japanese aristocracy, the Samurai, and which only at the end of the last century became a hobby for all.

Pun-ching. Picture by Sumie Buzen, 1808

An apple tree.
Bonsai should take their
inspiration from nature

15

2 BONSAI STYLES

No two bonsai are the same. However, in Japanese bonsai some typical shapes have evolved, all of which are found in nature. The most important ones to be able to recognise are as follows.

Japanese hawthorn *Crataegus carrieré*, cascade style—Kengai height approximately 85cm, age about 45 years

INDIVIDUAL TREES

Chokkan—formal upright

Strong, vertical trunk with pyramidal arrangement of branches stretching uniformly in all directions except forwards.

Moyogi—curved informal upright

Trunk winds round in curves that become smaller towards the top.

Shakan—slanting style

Similar to the windswept style (*see* p. 20) except that a Shakan has branches growing in all directions. Strong roots are exposed in the direction of incline.

Han-Kengai—semi cascade

This style does not cascade downwards from a rock, but juts out horizontally above a cliff.

Kengai—cascade or hanging style

Trunk and branches hang down over the edge of a pot, usually one that has been placed high up.

Japanese white pine *Pinus parviflora*, semi-cascade style—Han-Kengai width about 70cm, age about 85 years

Japanese larch *Larix leptolepis*, slanting style—Shakan height approximately 60cm, age about 50 years

Japanese white pine *Pinus parviflora*, curved informal upright style—Moyogi, height approximately 70cm, age about 75 years

Japanese black pine *Pinus thunbergi*, formal upright style—Chokkan height approximately 70cm, age about 80 years

TREES WITH SEVERAL TRUNKS, AND GROUP PLANTINGS

The Japanese have an aversion to even numbers. Only the number two is acceptable and numbers four and six in particular are avoided. Symmetry is not favoured, and this inevitably has a great influence upon bonsai shapes.

Sokan—twin trunk
Two trunks of differing thickness growing out of one root (father and son).

Sankan—triple trunk
Three trunks of differing thickness growing out of one root (father, mother, son).

Kabudachi—clump
The term used for all bonsai where several trunks grow from one root.

Ikada—raft style
Trunk buried horizontally in the ground with branches trained to give the effect of individual trees.

Netsuranari—raft from root, or sinuous, style
Several trunks growing from a root lying horizontally, producing the effect of a group of trees.

Yose-ue—multi-tree or group planting
Several miniature trees of greatly differing ages planted in a flat dish to give the appearance of a wood or forest glade.

Japanese red maple *Acer palmatum* 'Atropurpureum', raft style—Ikadabuki, height approximately 66cm, age about 45 years

18

Japanese white-barked beech
Fagus crenata,
triple trunk style—
Sankan
height
approximately 85cm,
age about 65 years

STYLES THAT MAY BE PLANTED SINGLY OR IN GROUPS

 Hokidachi—broom, or besom, style
Fan-shaped branches on an upright trunk to look like a giant broom.

 Fukinagashi—windswept style
Trunk at an angle with branches and twigs growing only in one direction—as if lashed by the wind.

 Bunjingi—literati style
Trunk or trunks growing upright or at a slight incline with no branches except at the top. An elegant shape.

 Ishitsuki—clinging-to-rock, or rock grown, style
Miniature tree growing above or on a rock, its roots firmly clasping the stone and reaching down into the richness of the soil.

Winter jasmine *Jasminum nudiflorum*, clinging-to-rock style—Ishitsuki height about 27cm, age about 35 years

Japanese grey-barked elm *Zelkova serrata*, broom (besom) style—Hokidachi, height about 80cm, age about 75 years

Japanese white pine *Pinus parviflora*, literati style—Bunjingi, height about 80cm, age about 65 years

This Japanese white pine *Pinus parviflora* combines two bonsai styles: windswept and clump = Fukinagashi-Kabudachi height approximately 72cm age about 85 years

Japanese grey-barked elm *Zelkova serrata*, group planting—Yose-ue
height approximately 60cm, age about 5–25 years

Japanese cedar *Cryptomeria japonica*, twin trunk style—Sokan
height approximately 65cm, age about 35 years

Needle juniper *Juniperus rigida*, group planting—Yose-ue
height approximately 90cm, age about 12–30 years

BONSAI GROUP PLANTINGS

In a bonsai group individual trees are arranged to create the effect of an unbroken group of trees.

All types of tree groups that are found naturally can be fashioned as bonsai groups. So it is possible to create dense, dark pine forests, light, airy deciduous woodlands, windswept coastal woods, small glades on plateau-land, and infinite variations.

Different perspectives can be worked out to create good effects; some bonsai groups appear quite close at hand as if in cinematic close-up, others suggest great depth, and others, coastal woods for example, are narrow and elongated. The age, shape and condition of the trees are also important characteristics.

The possibilities for shaping and arranging your group are as many and varied as there are models to choose from in nature. Your group planting will have succeeded only if you can capture the particular atmosphere unique to every group of trees. And to be able to recreate this atmosphere all you must do is observe a few rules when planning. Beginners will find group plantings an ideal place to start as they help to open your eyes to the great variety of tree and forest shapes around in the wild. They give pleasure right from the start as the miniature forest is quickly planted and, in a superficial sense, finished. You don't need years of work to see it completed and your creation can be corrected at any time subsequently, perhaps by removing individual trees, replacing some, or transferring some within the group. And since you use young trees, only between two and eight years old, the material you start with is not too costly. You can, if you obtain permission from the relevant authorities, collect your material yourself from the wild, but it is simpler, and probably in the better interests of conservation, to get your bonsai material in tree nurseries where you will find a great selection of saplings. As with single bonsai you should preferably look for small-leaved plants and for species that can tolerate a severe chop to the roots. This is often necessary because the plants will be grouped in very flat dishes and there won't be much room for the roots.

Try and make sure wherever possible that your trees are of the same stock or variety; than at least the common hereditary characteristics will ensure the same leaf size, colour and the development of trees of similar height. This will give your group of trees a more uniform appearance and harmonious effect.

Mixed woods look most attractive, but as time passes problems may arise in caring for them: the growth and cultural requirements of different trees can vary so much that the development of one species can upset that of another. So it is best to choose just one species for your bonsai forest. Maples, bamboos, beeches, spruces, hornbeams, needle junipers, larches, cedars, stewartias, elms and cypresses are all very suitable for planting as groups.

The best time for planting is the beginning of spping, before the buds open, because small plants will best tolerate their roots being cut at that season. It is also possible to start off your forest early in autumn, but the roots should be trimmed only moderately then.

Beech saplings, 2–5 years old, being prepared for planting as a group.
The roots are pruned by two-thirds.
A mixture of equal parts of loam and peat is formed into balls.

To make grouping easier, the roots are encapsulated in a mixture of peat and loam. The balls thus formed make it easy to place the trees in the desired positions.

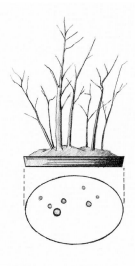

After filling the container with bonsai earth, moss is laid on top or seeds can be sown.

Sketch showing how the beech wood is planted

The soil mixture used for your bonsai forest is the same as that used for single bonsai (*see* p. 98).

Before planting anything, make a sketch showing where you are going to place each tree.

Individual trees should be carefully arranged: you could keep in mind the style of turn-of-the-century photographs, with the most important tree, superior in height and thickness of trunk, the father, in the foreground, the second most important, the mother, arranged near him, and the less important, like children in the group, placed around both father and mother. This allows the tree group to be divided into sub-groups, which lends your miniature forest a naturalness and depth. Plant all the larger trees towards the front, with the smaller ones at the back, to create an even greater illusion of depth. As you plant them, position the trees in such a way that any long branches point outwards. No tree should hide another. And remember that in any group the space you leave free is just as important as the trees themselves; it is space that helps create a proper landscape.

Before planting prepare your bonsai dishes in the normal way: put small pieces of plastic mesh over the drainage holes, cover the dish with gravel for drainage using a very thin layer since the dishes are very shallow; then add an equally thin layer of bonsai soil mix.

Plant the main trees first, then the others. It can be difficult to secure the individual trees in position, but either of the two following methods should help.

1 Pull wire through the drainage holes and secure the main trees to the bottom of the dish. Once these are firmly in position the neighbouring trees can be attached to the main ones. Don't forget to remove the wire after about six months.

2 Form the mass of roots of each plant into a ball by applying a moist mixture of loam and peat. You will thus give your trees enough weight to enable them to stand in place.

After the spaces between the trees have been filled in with bonsai soil mix press the soil down over the entire dish, particularly at the edges. Pieces of moss can be laid on top, the trees should be watered thoroughly, and then the dish should be placed somewhere sheltered. After four to six weeks you can gradually accustom your forest to the sun and apply small amounts of fertiliser.

Fifteen Japanese grey-barked elms, 5–20 years old, their roots pruned ready for planting; a suitable dish, soil, tools.

Firstly the three main trees are put in position on top of a thin drainage layer of soil and secured with wires pulled through the drainage holes.

Next, all the remaining trees are arranged to give the miniature forest as much depth as possible. Note with this arrangement that there are two tree groups, each forming a small triangle and together forming a large one.

After the container has been filled with bonsai compost, moss is laid on top.

The forest is now watered thoroughly and placed in a sheltered position.

Japanese grey-barked elm *Zelkova serrata*, group planting—Yose-ue, height approximately 60cm, age about 25 years

28

Hinoki cypress *Chamaecyparis obtusa*, group planting—Yose-ue, height approximately 58cm, age about 12–18 years

Far-Eastern charm of a miniature bamboo forest, about 53cm high

The miniature forest seen in close-up

Needle juniper *Juniperus rigida*, group planting—Yose-ue, height approximately 90cm, age about 12–30 years

32

Japanese grey-barked elm *Zelkova serrata*, group planting—Yose-ue, height approximately 80cm, age about 8–25 years

ROCK PLANTINGS

Bonsai arrangements using rocks follow two basic patterns: those with plants rooted on the rock and having no link with the earth in the dish, and those whose roots run down over the rock into the earth.

Good bonsai rock compositions are achieved when the plants, rocks and dishes form a natural-looking unity. To help you succeed in this, it is advisable to make a sketch, just as was suggested for the bonsai forests, so that you can see in what positions the trees and rocks will best complement one another. The main thing to consider is which quality of a rocky landscape you wish to recreate and which perspective you will select for it. Again, do you want your landscape to look as if it is close by or in the distance? These are considerations that will determine how you arrange the two basic elements of your bonsai. Rocks will look like giant cliff-faces if the trees on them are relatively much smaller, and they'll shrink to the size of rocky fragments if the trees dominate the scene.

The first case we'll look at is where trees are rooted on the rock, and secondly we'll consider trees which have their roots buried in the earth in the dish. There are in addition a great many variations of these two basic forms: for example, some roots may get their nutrition partly from the earth in the rock crevices and partly from the earth in the dish. The trees themselves may already have been fully shaped and wired before being positioned on the bonsai arrangement or only the first steps towards shaping may have been attempted.

Bonsai arrangements using stones allow your imagination to run riot and you can attempt almost any combination—although one thing to avoid is having rocks and plants of the same size because you'll end up with something that looks lifeless and unnatural.

Containers to use for rock plantings are usually shallow dishes of a subdued, restful colour.

Arranging a rock bonsai

The following method is recommended for rock plantings where the trees are not connected with the soil in the dish but are rooted on top or at the side of the rock, often several together on one rock.

Firstly, you have to choose your plants and stones. For your first attempt use trees that have already been trained, but it doesn't matter

The rock is prepared. All the necessary tools for shaping and arranging a rock planting lie alongside. Next the trees are held against the rock to work out which are the most effective positions.

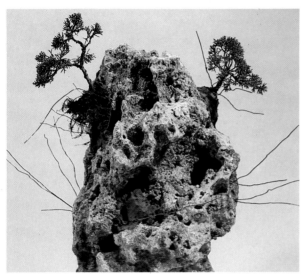

Starting from the top the trees are placed in the hollows that have been filled with the peat/loam mixture, and secured firmly.

When all the plants are secure, cover them with as much peat/loam mixture as possible.

Lay moistened pieces of moss on top and wire in place.

This particular rock planting stands in a shallow, water-filled dish, symbolising a lake over which a rock towers. Alternatively, the dish could be filled with silver sand.

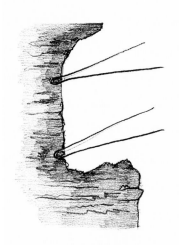

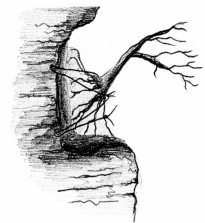

The wires are secured with pieces of lead in small holes drilled to the right and left of the rock hollows.

Before planting, smear the hollows with the moist peat/loam mixture and then secure the plants with wires.

Cover over with the same soil mixture and place pieces of moss on top.

whether those trees are young or old, or mame bonsai (*see* p. 50). Attractive stones can be found almost anywhere; choose ones with an interesting shape and strong colouring, so much more expressive than stones with an off-white or greyish tinge. Examine your find from every angle and ask yourself what it could become in your rocky landscape—could it symbolise a mountain, a rocky island in the sea, a rugged coastline falling steeply away? These particular images are very popular with bonsai-growers and you'll come across them repeatedly; they also occur as saikei (*see* p. 46). The stone should also have a rough surface with cavities and small hollows for attaching your plants.

Once you have decided which surface is to be the front, back, top and bottom of your stone, you will have to correct any problems with the surface you are going to stand the stone upon, either with a quick-drying cement or by sanding the underneath carefully with a grinding stone. You may also have to dig out the hollows with a stone chisel to make more room for soil and for the trees' roots.

Now gather together your trees and any complementary plant matter to go underneath, such as fresh moss, and a soil mixture made up of equal parts peat and loam moistened so that it will stick well to the rock. You will also need copper or aluminium wire, bonded adhesive or pieces of lead (fishing weights or printers' type), hammer and centre-punch, hairpin-shaped clips made from the wire, and possibly a drill with a 6mm masonry bit.

There are two ways of fixing the wires which will be used to secure the trees to the rock. You can drill holes to either side of the rock cavities, then push the U-shaped bits of wire in and keep them in place with a piece of lead hammered flat with the centre-punch and hammer (*see* above). However, it is probably easier if you make small loops from the wire and stick these to the rock with a bonded adhesive, then pull the securing wires through these loops.

Before finally carrying out the planting, the arrangement of the trees on the rock should be checked again, holding them up at the pre-selected sites. A point to remember when several types of plant are being used in the arrangement is that the laws of nature should be observed, using conifers higher up, and ferns and grasses lower down.

Next, the rock should be dampened with water and the hollows filled with a layer of the peat/loam mixture 1–2cm thick. Now the plants can be put in. Most of the earth should have been removed from the roots either by scratching it away with a stick or by washing it off. You can, of course, leave as much earth on the ball of roots as will go into the hollow.

Secure the plants with wires; as a general rule, don't cut away roots that stick out—spread them alongside on the rock. The entire root system should now be covered over with as thick a layer as possible of the peat/loam mixture. Now position the ground plants, fix in place with wires, and support with the moist-ened soil mixture; lastly place moist pieces of moss all over the top and secure with the prepared wire clips.

Stand the planted rock in a flat, oval dish with silver sand or water, and place it out of the wind in a semi-shaded spot. Bonsai rock plantings dry out easily, so you must spray them frequently so that they always feel moist. Try not to wash away any soil when spraying newly planted rocks. After about eight weeks you can give the first application of fertiliser and this should be in liquid form. This type of rock bonsai should not be replanted or the roots trimmed, but from time to time any soil that has been washed away should be replaced. Rock bonsai with plants rooted on the rock should be kept frost-free otherwise the roots may become dislodged from the stone.

Clinging-to-rock bonsai

A rock suitable for a clinging-to-rock bonsai, where the roots wrap themselves over the stone and sink into the soil in the dish.

Before adding the trees the rock should be smeared with a thin layer of peat and loam mixture.

With trees in position, the roots are arranged decoratively.

All the roots on the rock are covered with sphagnum moss or peat and wrapped around with strips of muslin.
Now place the rock planting in a dish.

If you want to have a root-over-rock bonsai you will need a plant with very long roots. You might like to select a well-rooted plant from a nursery, one that has been growing in a tall pot and so has developed long roots. You can then shape it into a bonsai before or after it has been placed over the stone. Another good source of long-rooted plants—though bear in mind the conservation laws—are small trees growing in highland regions.

If you would like to change a bonsai into a root-over-rock bonsai, the following method will help encourage the roots to grow particularly long. A lovely *Acer palmatum*, for example, can be transferred from a bonsai dish to a narrow, plastic bucket with drainage holes, roughly the height of the rock you have in mind: fill it with a looser soil than bonsai soil mix, preferably a sand/peat mixture, and here the plant's roots can grow as long as they like. Every three or four months cut off a strip about 5cm wide from the plastic bucket and remove the soil surrounding the upper parts of the roots to just below the brim. The roots still in the soil will now grow at a faster rate to replace the root mass that has been freed of the earth. Over a period of one or two years more and more strips of the bucket should be cut away and more roots laid bare until only 5–8cm of bucket are left. Now the bonsai should be prepared for planting on the stone. Plant it either in spring or in the autumn, although autumn is suitable only if the bonsai will be kept frost-free in the winter.

Before placing a tree on a stone the soil must first of all be completely removed from the roots either by scratching it away carefully with a stick or by dipping it repeatedly in water. This is so that the roots are easier to distribute over the stone. Individual roots that spoil the appearance—perhaps ones that are too thick—may be cut off if the plant can survive without them, but the other roots should not be trimmed.

Since root systems dry out easily they should now be submerged briefly in a loamy paste to give them a thin protective coating of loam. Next place the tree on the rock and secure with bast or thin raffia if necessary. Arrange the roots as decoratively as possible, the most attractive ones to the fore, and sink the root ends into the soil.

All root parts draping the rock should be covered with moist rough peat or sphagnum moss as an extra protection against drying out. The whole thing should then be wrapped around with muslin strips to attach it to the rock.

After this your bonsai will be weak, so like a newly repotted tree, it should be given special care and attention such as that described for the other rock plantings (*see* p. 37).

The muslin strips should always be kept slightly damp and should be removed only four to six months later, together with the peat and moss, after the plant has formed new roots in the dish.

Bonsai and rock together make a single unit and should be kept together when they are repotted after about two or three years.

Lengthening the roots

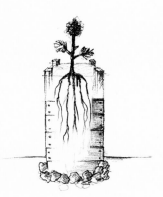

Method of accelerating the rate of growth of the roots in preparation for planting on a rock

Spiraea *Spiraea nitida* as a rock planting, height 20cm, age about 8 years

Chinese juniper *Juniperus chinensis*, a rock planting from China, height 65cm, age about 25 years

Golden Chinese juniper *Juniperus chinensis plumosa aurea*, a rock planting from Japan, height 60cm, age about 25 years

Trident maple *Acer buergerianum*, a particularly beautiful root-over-rock style, height 40cm, age about 45 years

Detail showing how the
roots grow down over
the rock into the soil

SAIKEI—MINIATURE LANDSCAPES

Saikei are miniature landscapes planted in shallow dishes to represent a piece of natural scenery—perhaps a strip of river, a waterfall in the mountains, a pine grove by the sea or a deciduous wood with pathways and streams.

Saikei have a long history if we include among the art those miniature landscapes depicted on thirteenth and fourteenth century scroll paintings; perhaps here there is a link with Chinese landscapes. The art of forming saikei was rediscovered only recently by Toshio Kawamoto, a Japanese bonsai master, who developed the art further. He founded a saikei school and made miniature landscapes very popular in Japan. In the West, too, saikei is becoming better known and has attracted much admiration from bonsai enthusiasts. Often different types of trees of varying sizes and growth patterns are planted together, although mostly, as with bonsai group plantings, only one species is used so that the grouping looks more natural.

Saikei are different from bonsai group plantings mainly in that not only trees are used but also rocks and various types of earth —sometimes even tiny houses, bridges, animals and figures, too. Good saikei formations work because the three basic elements, trees, rocks and earth combine in a harmonious way.

Unlike bonkai, which are miniature landscapes made up of only artificial materials, modelling clay and coloured sand without living plants, saikei have a lot in common with bonsai. The techniques for cultivating, shaping and caring for miniature trees to be used in saikei landscapes are the same as for bonsai. In saikei young bonsai plants, two or three years old, are used, and if at a later date they become too big for the miniature landscape, they can be relocated and trained as single bonsai. But saplings and less than successful mame bonsai (*see* p. 50) can also be planted. The various tree shapes you know already since they are the same as the bonsai ones—formal upright, cascade, raft style, rock planting, etc.

Stones have a very important function in saikei; all types of stones are suitable, but their shape will determine the essential character of the miniature landscape. Toshio Kawamoto has distinguished various sorts of stone; those suitable as mountains, islands, peninsulas, rivers, hills, 'lonely beach', etc. Saikei stones don't have to be absolutely perfect in shape because any part that is unpleasing to your eye can be covered with earth. The important things are type, shape and the quality of the top surface, and, of course, that the stones and trees go well together. Suitable containers for saikei are large, flat dishes of a neutral, tranquil colour.

You can use the same bonsai dishes as for bonsai forests and rock plantings: these will already have drainage holes in the bottom. Some people prefer wooden containers but these must first be treated with preservatives against damp and rot (making sure such treatment will not harm the plants). Some saikei dishes also have separate sections for use when creating maritime landscapes. Once you've gathered together your plants, stones, soil, mosses or other suitable ground plants, plus your dish, and maybe sand and gravel as well, you can start arranging as follows.

Cover the drainage holes on the bottom of the dish with plastic or wire netting, then scatter a very thin layer of soil mix over the bottom and place the individual trees in position. They will stand firmer if you make the roots into a ball first, using a wet mixture of loam and peat (*see* photo, p. 27). Now place the stones in the dish, keeping in mind an exact picture of how you want your landscape to look.

One basic principle to keep in mind is that you should place the tree and its associated stone with its middle point at the centre of the container if the two items are to be kept close together; often, however, you'll create greater depth if you push the stone a little to the rear. The stones should always be placed so that they complement the direction of growth of the trees.

Your miniature landscape really will resemble a piece of nature if you've balanced the heights of the trees and stones. A stone that is meant to be a rock, for example, will of course be correspondingly bigger than the trees. Once trees and stones are in their correct positions in your landscape, fill the spaces in between with bonsai soil mix; it is perhaps a good idea to sprinkle small mounds of soil round the trees and stones first and then cover the rest of the area. Don't make the soil layer too thick; it's an important part of the shape of your landscape, enriching it with a gentle uneven pattern of tiny hills and valleys. Lastly, water your saikei thoroughly and if you wish cover it with pieces of moss or other suitable ground plants. Again make sure that everything remains in proportion; grasses shouldn't be as tall as a man in relation to the miniature trees.

Your newly planted saikei should be placed in a sheltered spot out of the wind and in addition to watering it should be sprayed once daily. Then continue to care for it in the same way as a rock planting (*see* p. 37). During winter saikei need to be kept free of frost and at a temperature of between 0° and 7°C.

Saikei, height 35cm, width 30cm, age about 12 years, a rocky gorge created with Japanese cedars and stones

Saikei, height 25cm, width 45cm, age 8–15 years,
Japanese cedars, a group of trees on an alpine meadow

Saikei, height 28cm, width 35cm, age 15 years,
Japanese cedars, a wooded gorge in autumn

Saikei, height 35cm, width 40cm, age 12–15 years,
cryptomerias, needle junipers, a small rocky landscape

Saikei, height 23cm, width 32cm, age 12–15 years,
Japanese cedars, a coastal landscape in autumn colours

MAME BONSAI

Mame bonsai are small enough to be held comfortably in the palm of the hand. They should not exceed 8–15cm in height and, with few exceptions, their care and shaping is the same as for their larger counterparts. You can obtain mame bonsai by collecting plants from the wild if you have permission, by cultivating them from cuttings and seeds, by growing them from off-shoots or by buying them from bonsai nurseries.

Mame need to be grown for between three and five years to shape the tree sufficiently to warrant the name. It is possible to start with seedlings 3–5cm tall, easily found in woods and parks at the foot of large trees. Many of these tiny off-shoots are an interesting shape even at this stage. Of course, mame should be miniature versions of the original tree, not some grotesquely deformed plant. You could shape a zelkova like a broom, cryptomerias as pillars; and pines make good mame with all the characteristics of the original species.

Spring is the best time of year to go looking for suitable plant material. Once you have permission, dig the plant out carefully without damaging the root fibres, but remove the tap-root. Leave some earth on the roots and wrap the plant in damp moss or moistened newspaper so that it doesn't dry out. The choice of dish is very much a matter of taste, the only important feature being a sufficiently large drainage hole in the bottom. The correct soil mixture is also vital for the survival of your plant. You can use the tried and tested bonsai soil mixtures, although the mix should be very fine. Mame bonsai, and those that are being trained as such, should be watered at least three times daily, more often in summer, depending on heat and wind, because the two or three tablespoons of earth they need dry out very quickly.

One easy way of watering is to immerse your tree in water until no more air bubbles rise to the top.

Pruning is the most important technique to master in the shaping of a mame bonsai, since the plants are too small to allow much wiring. Start by pruning back the young trees you have collected to one or two buds. Repeat until the plants begin to look more interesting. Then encourage some of the tiny branches to grow, and nip off the more dominant ones with your fingers.

Flowering cherry *Prunus serrulata*,
height approximately 12cm, age about 8 years

cutting branches and roots

Covering the drainage hole with plastic netting

Adding a soil drainage layer

After the tree has been planted press the earth down with a wooden stick or with your fingers

Water thoroughly

Shaping a Moyogi style

Spring, before the first pruning

Autumn the same year, after the first pruning

Autumn the following year, after the second spring pruning

Autumn of the third year

If you want to achieve a mame with descending branches you can either bind branches with copper wire or tie string round the container and pull the branches down as far as possible with some twine and tie it to the string.

Apply fertiliser sparingly. Diluted liquid fertiliser is best for mame, and it should be applied as with normal bonsai once a week, *after* watering from late spring to autumn. Sometimes, because mame can be so very small, it is best to inject your fertiliser through the drainage hole at the bottom of the dish.

After a while all plants exhaust their soil, and mame are particularly prone to this since they grow in only two or three tablespoonfuls of it. They therefore have to be repotted more frequently than larger bonsai, and at the repotting the roots should be pruned by a third. With large-leaved species you should remove about half the leaves so that they do not demand too much of the newly trimmed root system.

All foliage must be sprayed daily, and at first the small plant must be placed somewhere that is sheltered from sun and wind, until about a week later when it can be introduced to the sun.

The location you choose for your mame is the same as for normal bonsai and instructions regarding its care and cultivation are no different from those for normal bonsai. Here too a 'completed' bonsai is the product of many years' perseverance and patient tending.

Mame may not live to be hundreds of years old but they can survive three generations if well looked after. Sometimes, despite all care and attention, your mame will grow too big, in which case you can shape it into a normal sized

Tying down the branches to create a downward effect

bonsai.

In Japan the creation of mame is very popular, and astonishingly high prices are offered for them.

Injecting fertiliser

Mame bonsai beautifully displayed on a Japanese bonsai rack. The deciduous trees are about 25 years old, the conifers about 30–45 years old.

Mame bonsai, height 6–12cm, age 6–10 years

Mame bonsai, height about 8–18cm, age about 8–15 years

A small selection of mame bonsai containers ranging from 4–15cm
Opposite: Ideas for bonsai are found in nature. A pear tree.

3 CULTIVATION

Let us look now at what comprises suitable 'raw material' for developing a bonsai. In fact, almost any plants that flourish in temperate climates can be shaped into miniature trees, but trees and shrubs are particularly suitable. Even then it is advisable to select species that have small leaves, small flowers and a compact growth. You'll find a selection of popular bonsai species in the Table on pages 182ff.

Propagation methods for bonsai are the same as for other trees, but you may prefer to collect suitable seedlings from the wild or buy from a nursery. Remember, if collecting from the wild, to consult the appropriate authority before removing any plant.

BONSAI FROM SEEDS

Some really lovely bonsai can be grown from seed provided you have the necessary patience to wait the five, six or seven years it may take for the typical bonsai shape to emerge. Growing from seed enables you to enjoy, right from the start, the development of your miniature tree and to see how your influence can create whatever effect you desire. Nearly all trees can be cultivated from seed, the most popular among the conifers being yews, spruces, pines, larches and firs, and among broadleaves maples, birches, beeches, pyracanthas, ginkgos, pomegranates, hornbeams, Japanese beeches and zelkovas.

In the autumn when you go for walks in the fields and woods you will find many sorts of seeds from which to grow your seedling back at home. Everyone remembers sycamore wings from their childhood, but just as a reminder all berries, fruits and nuts carry seeds, for example the brilliant red berries of pyracanthas, and yews, beech mast, acorns, hazelnuts, pomegranates and fir cones.

Public gardens often include particularly beautiful and sometimes rare trees; you may be lucky enough to obtain permission to collect ginkgo, cedar or cypress seeds here. If you can't be bothered to gather your own seeds you can of course buy 'bonsai seeds' ready packed; but don't be deceived by the pictures of bonsai on the packet—all you get inside is the material to start you off.

The various types of seed differ enormously in weight, size, appearance and in the type of seed-case, and there are correspondingly different methods of sowing the seeds to germinate them.

Some seeds, such as beech, oak, euonymus, fir, pine and spruce, are ready to germinate as soon as they have been gathered and so can be sown straightaway, or they can be kept in a cool, dry place (in a jar or plastic container) until you want to sow them.

Other types of seed, such as the common beech, although they too are ready to germinate immediately, must be kept in some moist sand prior to use otherwise they will lose the ability to germinate.

Many types of seed are still not capable of germination even when the fruit ripens in the autumn; they need a resting period first. Seeds of this sort must be stratified for germination to

sow the seeds

cover with sand or earth

press down with a small piece of wood

water thoroughly

commence, and this means layering them in moist sand and keeping them cool and frost-free. The period of dormancy may last from six to twelve months. Seeds belonging to this category include mountain maple, other Japanese maples, cotoneasters, juneberry or amelanchier, hornbeams, japonicas, hawthorns, sea buckthorn, hollies and junipers.

Before sowing, the seeds should be put in water for a day or two to let them swell up and allow the preliminary germination to take place. Seeds with hard outer husks should be scratched as well, as this makes germination more certain. I would also recommend a caustic treatment for your seeds using one of the proprietary wet or dry fungicides as this will protect the seeds from common seedling diseases such as damping off and root rot.

Seeds can be sown in spring, late summer and in autumn. I find Jiffy pots particularly good for sowing, especially for single seeds, or I use shallow, plastic seed trays about 10cm deep. Bonsai dishes or wooden boxes are other possibilities, as are any simple containers with drainage holes. Cover the holes first with plastic mesh before filling with soil. A mixture of equal parts peat and sand should be placed in your container, or you can use commercially available cactus soil; rhododendrons and other plants that like acid soil will do best with pure peat. Add enough soil till it is about 3cm below the rim of the container, then sieve another layer of the same soil roughly 1cm thick on top. Press the earth down with a small bit of wood then add the seeds, spaced well apart. Sieve some more soil to cover the seeds or use fine sand—this final covering layer should be very thin, only about twice as deep as the diameter of the seeds. Press down again gently with the piece of wood, then water with a fine mist spray. Cover the container with a sheet of glass and stand it out of direct sunlight; in autumn make sure also that frost can't get at it. Many of your seeds may not sprout because they are still 'resting'; in such cases germination will have been abandoned till the following year. Note that prolonged dormancy of this sort can be curtailed in some species of maple simply by a one-off increase in temperature. That is why the sown seeds must be kept in a shaded position where the sun cannot heat up the earth too much; choose a place where a ground temperature of no more than 15°C—suitable for all types of seeds—is guaranteed.

As soon as the seed leaves (cotyledons) begin to show, place a bit of wood under the glass sheet to let fresh air in to the young seedlings. The sheet of glass can be removed completely once the first true leaves appear.

In early summer the young seedlings can be fed with small amounts of fertiliser for the first time. Once they are about 10cm tall repot them into normal flowerpots and gradually introduce them to the sun. Depending on the species, bonsai shaping can be started after one or two years.

BONSAI FROM CUTTINGS
You don't need so much patience to grow bonsai from cuttings as you do to grow them from seeds.

Cuttings can be defined as parts of plants, without roots of their own, that are cut from healthy, vigorous parent plants and placed in soil to take root.

Most kinds of plants can be propagated from cuttings, including cryptomerias (Japanese cedars), firs, yews, junipers and cypresses among the conifers, and maples, azaleas, cotoneasters, pomegranates, jasmines, olive-trees, elms, willows and zelkovas among broadleaves. You can of course use the branches that you prune from your bonsai each year as cuttings to produce new plants for training as bonsai.

Many cuttings will also produce roots easily in water-glass, willows and zelkovas being two examples.

Cuttings for propagation can be taken at any time during the year but they are best when the

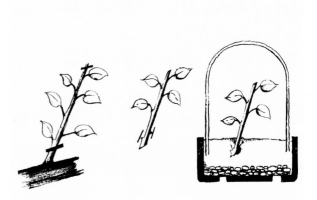

Separate the cutting from the parent plant and cut back the main shoot

Remove lower leaves

Plant in prepared pot and water thoroughly

current year's shoots are sufficiently mature for the cutting process. As a guide, cuttings from deciduous trees should be taken from the very beginning of summer when they are medium-hard. Conifer cuttings must always be fully mature and so can be taken either shortly before the leaf buds appear at the beginning of spring or in early autumn when the young shoots have become sufficiently woody and firm.

Cuttings taken in spring will develop roots more quickly than those taken in autumn.

Rooting powders can encourage roots to grow even better. Use one of the many proprietary brands that are on the market and dip the ends of your cuttings in it before planting in pots.

Cuttings taken from broadleaves should have at least four to six pairs of leaves, and so they are likely to be about 4–10cm long, depending on the species and the distance between sets of leaves. Using a pair of scissors or a very sharp knife make a cut below a leaf joint on the parent plant. Cut off the soft tip of the shoot and also remove any lower leaves that would be pushed into the soil when planting, as they'd only rot.

Without exception, the only cuttings used from conifers are the tips of young shoots. Trees with particularly long new shoots, such as *Chamaecyparis, Juniperus* and *Thuja* spp., can be trimmed back and the lower needles carefully pulled away.

The same containers suggested for sowing seeds can be used for cuttings, i.e. flowerpots, seed trays, bonsai dishes and wooden boxes. Fill the dish with a mixture of equal parts peat and sand to just below the rim, press the earth down

gently; then push the cuttings in about 3cm, making sure you leave enough space between each cutting. Now water thoroughly. To prevent evaporation, cover with plastic film stretched over wire hoops and attached to the dish with a rubber band or raffia.

Now place your mini-propagator in a bright spot away from direct sunlight. Remember, cuttings need a constant temperature of 15–18°C to root well. Bear in mind that your cuttings will need to be sprayed several times daily in the first few weeks, less later on, to stop the leaves wilting. The earth should be kept slightly moist at all times—never allowed to dry out.

Once rooting has taken place (obvious by the growth of new shoots), the plastic film can be lifted during the day an hour at a time to harden off the plants and gradually you can build up to leaving the cover off altogether. Once the young plants have developed a small ball of roots they should be planted individually in pots. After another four weeks in a shaded spot the plants can gradually be introduced to the sun and they can also be given fertiliser for the first time. During the winter make sure frost cannot attack your trees.

After one or two years, depending on species, you can begin training your bonsai.

GROUND LAYERING METHOD OF PROPAGATION

It is possible to create bonsai from most shrubs by pulling a lower branch down into the ground and pinning it in place, but with trees, only those with low hanging branches will be successful: examples are magnolias, pines, forsythias, weigelas, and juneberry.

Bend the branch down, removing any leaves and needles from the area that will be below the earth. Make one or two lengthwise incisions in this part about 4cm long on the underside; this makes it easier for the roots to form. Now bury the branch about 10cm down in the earth and keep it moist at all times. After roots have formed, this branch can be cut away from the parent plant.

Shoots on shrubs can be encouraged to produce roots by packing earth or peat round them. Any plants produced should be separated from the parent plant either in autumn after the leaves have dropped off or the following spring before growth has resumed.

Two ground layering methods for producing young plants

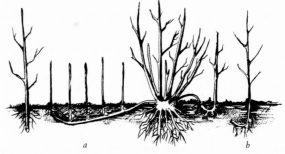

In (a) shoots are laid horizontally on the ground and covered with earth. The new plants will have straight ends to their roots. In (b) shoots are sunk into the ground and twisted, then secured in this position with a hook. The end of the branch should point upwards. The new plants that develop will have curved ends to their roots.

BONSAI FROM THE WILD

In years gone by many people in Japan used to take themselves off to the mountains in spring to find suitable bonsai, and they often brought home with them some really lovely specimens. Even today, showing years of tender loving care, many of the trees collected in those times can still be seen at annual bonsai exhibitions.

Today the Japanese can go collecting only with the permission of the appropriate forestry authorities, and even then they are obliged to replace any seedling they pick with one from a tree nursery. And before digging up any plant the permission of the authority or owner must have been sought. This is particularly important in the case of a relatively established young tree, whereas young seedlings which are to be found all over the place beneath large trees might be removed without too much damage to the environment.

Before collecting from the wild you should gain the permission of the landowner if you intend removing any material, and make sure you are up-to-date with information regarding protected species. Your chances of successfully replanting your find will be good if you go collecting at the beginning of spring; plants will not have begun to grow again and so can still tolerate a change of site quite well. Take with you a small spade, a sharp knife or secateurs, a couple of plastic boxes, newspaper and some water. That way you'll be able to dig up your specimen with as much root and soil attached as possible, and be able to wrap it in damp newspaper to stop it drying out and get it home safely. I would go so far as to say that almost every plant can be trained as a bonsai, but it is true that you'll make life a lot easier for yourself if you dig up only those specimens that show an interesting and vigorous growth. Seedlings about 10–20cm high are suitable material and should present no problems for further cultivation as they still have a compact ball of roots and can be taken out of the ground easily. The older a tree seedling is, the more sensitively it will react to being dug up, because it takes in its nutrients mainly through the fine fibrous roots that are so numerous along the root tips—these tend to get left behind in the soil when older plants are dug up.

With older trees it is best to remove any problematic or overlong branches from the crown of the tree first, then mark out a circle on the ground round the trunk roughly the same size as the diameter of the crown of the tree. Make a narrow trench along this line with your spade, cutting through any roots you come across with your knife or secateurs. Gradually go deeper with your ditch to form a semicircle underneath corresponding in size to the radius of the ball of roots extracted, and cut through the thick tap-root. Now carefully remove your tree from the ground, keeping the ball of earth intact (*see* illustration, p. 127).

Pack the rootball in damp newspaper or in damp moss which you'll normally find near at hand. At home plant your young tree in loose soil in the garden or put it in a large pot with a good drainage layer and a mixture of equal parts peat/sand. The crown of the tree should be trimmed once more so as not to overburden the roots.

Now place the plant somewhere fairly shaded and out of the wind. You could perhaps construct a plastic roof for your little tree, as suggested for your seedlings and cuttings, because under it the tree will recover more quickly and produce new fibrous roots and shoots. Whatever protection from evaporation you have provided may be removed after six to eight weeks, and the tree can gradually be acclimatised to its environment. After one or two years the roots should be cut and the tree repotted into a bonsai dish.

GRAFTING

Grafting is the horticultural technique of binding together different parts of a plant so that they fuse into a unit that continues to live. It involves grafting a piece of one plant, a one or two year old branch, known as the 'scion', on to another plant usually of the same species, known as the 'stock'. The stock has the task of forming the roots and the lower trunk, and the scion will form the crown of the tree and the upper trunk. The fused plant pieces form a new plant although at the same time each retains its individuality. This can clearly be seen in the different types of shoots above and below the grafting point, the varying thicknesses of trunk, and very often the different patterns on the bark of the scion and stock. For the bonsai enthusiast grafting has a variety of uses—he can use the technique to cultivate his tree, then to improve it and again to maintain it. Trees whose roots have been damaged can be prevented from dying by grafting techniques; flowering trees can in the same way acquire flowers of different hues.

Plants that with other methods would be difficult or impossible to cultivate can be propagated by grafting. Experience has shown, for example, that white pines have grown much more quickly after a graft; that is, with the aid of a different root. That is why in Japan nearly all white pines are grafted on to black pines.

Another advantage of grafting is in producing a variety of plant strains, for although the plant will always correspond to the scion in appearance and colour, seeds sown from the same plant may produce a great number of varieties.

However, there are also some disadvantages to grafting. The spot where the graft was carried out may not seal up attractively and unsightly shoots may start growing below the spot. The grafting technique itself needs skill and a certain amount of experience.

The most important types of grafting as far as the bonsai-grower is concerned are lateral grafting, wedge grafting, crown or rind grafting, bud grafting and branch grafting.

As a general rule plants are grafted at the beginning of spring before active growth has resumed. However, evergreen trees may also be grafted in late summer.

The following are bonsai species usually cultivated by grafting: apricot trees (in fact all types of fruit trees), wisterias, prunus-leaved hollies, red-leaved maples, japonicas, yeddo spruces, thick-barked black pines, and white pines.

Lateral grafting
This is carried out in summer and is applied chiefly to evergreen broadleaves and conifers in order to cultivate new plants.

The point where the graft is made should be as low down as possible on the lower trunk area so that it does not show up later on; if possible it should be hidden by earth. Cut the scion into a wedge about 3–5cm long, make a slanting incision of the same length on the trunk of the stock and insert the scion. Tie the scion to the stock with raffia and seal the grafting point with grafting wax (used for all types of graft), as this will stop the wound drying out and prevent water and pests from entering.

New growth from the scion the following year will tell you the graft has taken, at which point the stock should be cut away at an angle above the grafting point. If you do not want to use this method to create an entirely new tree, but perhaps only to insert a branch on a trunk

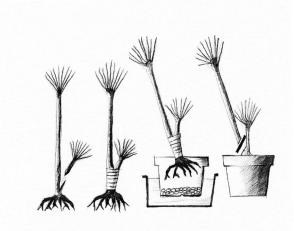

With a lateral graft, insert the scion into the slit on the stock, tie in position with raffia and seal the graft with grafting wax. Plant at an angle in a pot so that the grafted part will later form a tree in an upright position. Either stand in water for about ten minutes or water thoroughly. After the graft has taken, i.e. when you notice new growth, cut away the stock.

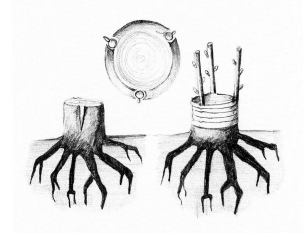

For a crown (or rind) graft you must cut horizontally through the trunk of the stock, then make slits in the bark 3–5cm long. Insert the ready-prepared scions behind the bark.

that seems too long, then remember to keep one side shorter on the scion when you're shaping the end into a wedge. This shorter side should lie next to the trunk when you insert it into the stock so that the scion will stick out from the trunk with a natural curvature (*see* illustrations above).

Crown, or rind, grafting and wedge grafting

Wedge grafting is attempted by bonsai experts only on fairly thin branches and trunks. If a trunk is more than 3cm thick the crown, or rind, grafting method is preferred.

Crown, or rind, grafting enables you to form multiple trunks, or to create anew rather elderly trees with a sound root system. An inferior or damaged crown can be repaired by removing the crown of the tree from the stock and inserting new branches.

With crown grafting the scion has a much smaller diameter than the stock. First of all the stock has to be sawn through neatly and smoothed off with a knife—this helps the cut to heal better. Next make a vertical incision 2–5cm long down the side. Gently tap the two folds of bark until they come loose then insert the ready-prepared, pre-cut scion. Using the same technique several scions can be arranged simultaneously round the trunk.

Secure the grafted area with raffia to keep the scions firmly in place, then apply wax both here and to the cut surface of the stock.

Wedge grafting entails making a slit in the

stock about 3cm deep parallel to the direction of growth of the trunk. Then insert at the side either one scion, 5–7cm long, previously sharpened into a wedge, or two scions one at each edge.

After securing with raffia, once again seal the graft with grafting wax. Wedge grafting enables you to insert new branches.

Bud grafting

With bud grafting, instead of a scion, only a small piece of bark with a well-formed heel is cut from the scion and inserted in the stock. This heel is the dormant bud lying at the join between the trunk and the leaf axil. This form of grafting is particularly good for inserting new branches.

The best time of year for bud grafting is summer, when the bark, complete with heel, will easily come away from the trunk. The bud should always be taken from the current year's

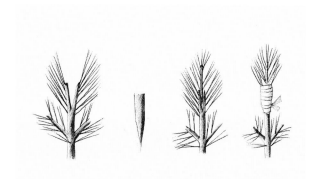

For wedge grafting make a slit about 2–3cm deep down the middle of the stock then insert the scion, previously sharpened at the end into a wedge shape. Wrap raffia round the grafted area and seal with wax.

growth area. Choose a fairly cool, rainy kind of day as this will help prevent the graft from drying out too quickly. Using a sharp grafting knife, make a T-shaped cut in the stock. Make the vertical cut first, about 2cm long, through to the xylem and not any deeper, then make the horizontal cut. Now loosen the bud from the scion, leaving a piece of bark about 1cm in diameter round the heel. If there is a leaf with the heel, remove it and only leave the leaf-stalk attached.

Using a knife, carefully peel back the bark of the T shape, open up the bark flaps and slide the heel in from above, using the leaf stalk as a lever if necessary. Then secure the graft with raffia or a rubber band, leaving the heel free. The graft will have taken once the leaf stalk has fallen off and a new branch has grown the following spring.

Bud grafting is particularly suited to fruit trees, such as apricot, cherry and peach, as well as roses. For the bonsai grower this technique is to be particularly recommended if he wants to turn a dioecious plant into a monoecious one, e.g. as with sea buckthorn and prunus-leaved holly. These plants form fruits only if both the male and female tree are present. By inserting a bud from a male, non fruit-bearing plant into a female, you can develop a tree that will fertilise itself and produce fruits.

Branch grafting

In this case the scion is not cut off straightaway; instead it is left attached to the parent plant for as long as it takes to fuse with the stock. This type of graft is suitable for all species of bonsai and is often carried out on the one plant, that is with

Cut a T-shape in the bark and fold back the flaps for inserting the heel of the scion. Secure in place with raffia, leaving the heel free.

firmly with raffia or a rubber band, before sealing with grafting wax. The graft won't take till perhaps late autumn of the same year, assuming the graft was carried out in the spring. Only then should the scion be separated from the parent plant, the cut being made as close as possible to the stock to keep the swelling small. The wound will heal better and more quickly if wax is applied. You can prepare your tree for branch grafting by letting a branch grow near the spot where you want one and later on bending it down for grafting.

General advice on grafting
With conifers and evergreens the scions are removed from the parent plant directly before the grafting; with deciduous trees you must wait till growth has ceased in autumn and winter,

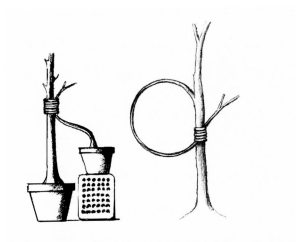

A new branch is grafted on to the trunk either from a separate plant or from the original one. With all forms of grafting plant parts will only fuse together if their cambium layers lie very close to one another. These layers lie just beneath the bark.

both scion and stock part of the same plant.

The drawings below give two examples, one showing how to attach a new branch to the trunk, and the other how to add a thinnish branch to a thicker one. Firstly cut away a strip of bark about 3cm long both from the stock and the scion, making sure that the cut sections match up well. Place them together and secure

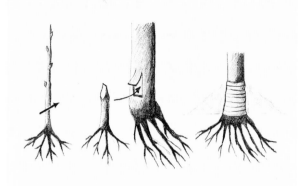

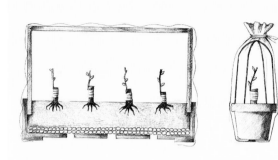

Root grafting involves taking the lower part of a young plant and inserting it at the side of a rather older plant. With this method you can replace dead roots and fill out any root system that has grown one-sided.

Two ways of protecting grafted plants till new parts begin to grow.

before cutting the scions. Choose a frost-free day. Stick them in damp sand and keep in a cool place out of reach of frost.

Usually scion and stock are selected from the same species of plant to ensure the graft will take. Bonsai growers can carry out all the techniques described with a sharp knife—no other tool is necessary.

It is very important to carry out all grafts quickly and with the highest degree of cleanliness to stop any bacteria getting into the wound. That is why it is also important not to touch the wounds with your fingers.

After grafting stand your plant somewhere out of the wind where temperatures are constant—in a hotbed propagator or under a plastic film wrap (*see* illustrations above).

After the graft has taken, as shown by new growth from the scion, the plant should gradually be acclimatised to normal environmental conditions. Remove the raffia after another year has passed.

Start in spring by making a slit 3–5cm long, working from bottom to top, in the branch selected for air-layering (*see* illustration below) then daub hormone rooting powder on to the slit to encourage roots to form. Stuff a bit of moss or a small stone into the slit to stop the flap of bark growing any more, then encase the whole area with a handful of sphagnum moss or peat. Wrap a piece of plastic film round the moss and seal the ends tightly with insulating tape to keep air out.

In a lot of cases, willows and privets, for example, roots form after only six weeks. Rhododendrons and beeches take about twice as long. With conifers you'll have to be patient for between one and two years before the first roots appear.

When enough roots have formed you may remove the plastic bag, and cut off the new plant and put it in a pot. Then it should be treated as a newly potted bonsai.

Air-layering on a parent plant

BONSAI BY AIR-LAYERING TECHNIQUES

Particularly beautiful branches of trees and shrubs can be encouraged to produce roots by the technique known as air-layering. One advantage of this method of propagation is that training can be started even on the parent plant. Choose branches not more than 3–5cm in diameter because with thicker branches there is less likelihood of roots forming.

The following are plants that respond well to air-layering: all maples, azaleas, beeches, cedars, spruces, forsythias, pyracanthas, pomegranates, wisterias, camellias, quinces, rhododendrons, elms, junipers, willows and zelkovas.

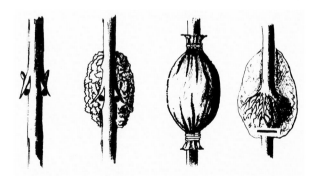

Tongue-shaped incision wedged with small stones

Area covered with damp moss and . . . plastic bag wrapped round it

Branch removed from parent plant after roots have developed

BONSAI TRAINING ON YOUNG PLANTS

The earlier you start to train a young plant the less drastic measures you will have to take later on. Young plants, at least two or three years old, cultivated from seeds, cuttings or by other methods of propagation, or collected from the wild, are all suitable bonsai material. They should be about 15–20cm tall, have a pencil-thick trunk and an adequate root formation. Then they can be transplanted. First of all, carefully brush away the earth from the roots and cut them back by a third of their total length. It is important when repotting that the pot is big enough to let the roots lie flat and distributed evenly in all directions. As described on page 106, a successful bonsai should look solid, firmly rooted in the earth, and that is only possible if the visible roots grow in every direction. It doesn't matter if they are of varying thickness or if the gaps between them vary, but they must never cross over. Take time over the training of the trunk area because it is a very important element in the overall effect of your bonsai and only limited improvements can be carried out later on. Tap-roots, such as those produced by pines and junipers, disturb the way roots are distributed and should be removed completely, provided there are enough fibrous roots. But if the plant has formed only a small root network you should cut back the tap root by only two-thirds at the most.

Pot your tree in a mixture of one part coarse sand and one part peat, or John Innes No 1. Leave for a few weeks in a protected, semi-shaded spot, then accustom it to the sun, and after about six weeks add fertiliser for the first

A Japanese maple after 4, 6, 8 and 15 years

time.

The best time for repotting is spring. Young plants should be repotted every two years and gradually be accustomed to bonsai soil. The various bonsai styles are achieved by trimming and wiring, but before you begin any training, you must have a clear idea of how you want your miniature tree to look in the end.

Spring is the right time for trimming and it is usually begun in the second year. It involves removing all buds and shoots growing in a direction you don't want. Nip out the buds and cut off the shoots with a pair of sharp scissors, in each case above a leaf axil.

If you remove the main shoot, the tip of the plant, you will allow more side shoots to grow. Your plant will grow more compactly if you regularly prune all the shoots, not only the main one.

Most deciduous trees can be trained without wiring because the right cut will determine the direction in which the side shoots will grow. The tip of each bud points in the direction in which a new branch would grow if the branch is cut off above the bud. (In a tiny, dormant bud

Training a seedling into a Moyogi style

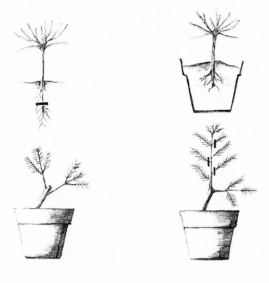

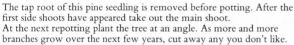

The tap root of this pine seedling is removed before potting. After the first side shoots have appeared take out the main shoot.
At the next repotting plant the tree at an angle. As more and more branches grow over the next few years, cut away any you don't like.

Once the tree is 3–5 years old you can start wiring it to produce its final form. When wiring the trunk make sure the branches are as shown in the illustration.
Now repot the pine into a bonsai dish.

the new branch would be undetectable to the naked eye.)

Gradually the tree will acquire a shape and you will be able to decide what kind of styles are possible. General instructions are given on page 18, and special instructions for a Moyogi style will be found above and on pages 52 and 75.

If you want to create a broom style, you must only remove the main shoot when the tree is as tall as you want it, because once you have cut the main shoot the height of the trunk is fixed forever. Now all the lateral shoots will be able to develop symmetrically, giving the appearance

of added thickness to the trunk. In the years that follow, with constant pruning back, the crown of the tree will produce new shoots (*see* illustrations p. 72).

After three or four years you can set about wiring the trunk and main branches—this is often essential with conifers.

After five or six years the young plant, now grown into a young miniature tree, should be placed in a bonsai dish.

Training a young plant into a broom style

After pruning the roots place the tree in a pot. Remove its tip if the trunk is as tall as you want it. By constantly trimming back the shoots you will gradually see a nicely shaped crown emerging. For one or two months before spring growth begins tie the branches together with string like a giant broom—this will stop the branches growing too horizontally and thus help create the typical broom shape.

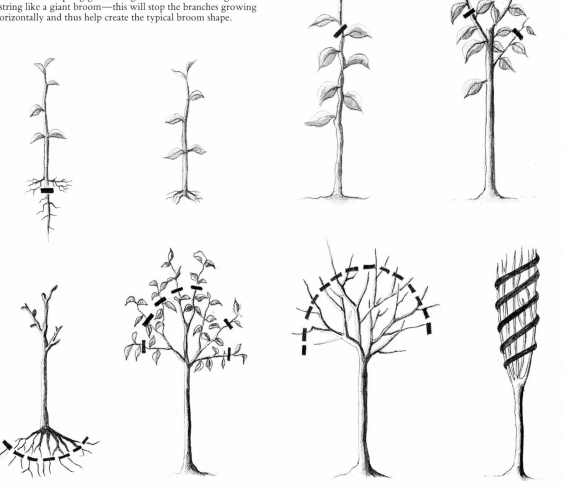

Zelkova carpinifolia
Caucasian zelkova
broom style—Hokidachi
height 30cm,
age about 15 years.
A fascinating little tree in
its autumnal splendour

BONSAI FROM NURSERIES

Nearly all the plants you can buy in nurseries and garden centres can be trained as bonsai, but particularly suitable are slow-growing species with compact growth and small leaves (*see* Table, p. 182). The best time for starting bonsai-training on a nursery tree is the beginning of spring, shortly before growth starts, and then again in autumn, after the trees have shed their leaves, become dormant, and the fruits have ripened.

When choosing your nursery tree bear in mind the eventual form you are aiming at. Look at the position of the branches and how thick they are; the individual branches should get thinner towards the top.

If you scratch away some of the earth round the trunk with your fingers, you can check the trunk really is attractive and whether it tapers away towards the top. Check also whether it is bent or flawed in any way, because none of these things is easy to correct later on.

If you select a container-grown tree get it home then cut the container as low down as possible so that you can easily remove the earth around the roots of the tree; if the roots are simply wrapped in a plastic bag then loosen it to get at them.

Next tidy the tree up a bit, get rid of any dead and insignificant little branches. With conifers pull off any needles and short shoots growing directly on the trunk. This will enable you to get a better view of your tree, to follow the linear flow of its trunk and branches and judge to which bonsai style it is best suited. Before going ahead and cutting off too much from a branch,

cover it up first with your hand and decide whether or not it is important for the overall effect. Cut the branches off directly at the trunk so that the scar lies as flush as possible. Fairly thick branches should be removed with a pair of concave scissors, the cut surfaces being sealed with wax to promote better healing.

The following rules may help with attaining the right proportions when training your tree. The lower third of the trunk is usually kept free of branches, because this gives it more impact. The main branches dominate the middle third and smaller ones the top third, becoming more and more fine and short the nearer you get to the top. Detailed information on trimming branches can be found on page 80.

After making appropriate cuts to shape your tree, repot it in a bonsai dish, having trimmed the roots by one third (*see* Potting and Repotting, p. 127).

Attacking your tree in these ways will have severely weakened it, so I would recommend postponing any wiring until the plant has grown new roots, a sign that it has recovered. Finally place the tree in a semi-shaded spot, out of the wind, and treat as a newly repotted tree for the first few weeks.

Training a nursery tree into a Kengai style

The blue Atlantic cedar shown
Cedrus atlantica glauca
height 55cm, age 8 years,
is particularly suited for
training into a Moyogi style.

Superfluous branches were first
removed and the two lower
branches prepared for jinning
(*see* p. 96). Two-thirds of the
root ball was cut away, the tree
was then wired and secured
firmly in a dish.

A Chokkan style from a nursery tree

a) *Juniperus chinensis* 'Monarch' a four-year-old juniper before training into the formal upright style.
b) Trunk and branches cleaned up, and any unwanted branches cut away with scissors.
c) Trunk and branches after wiring, bent into the required direction.
d) The young bonsai standing in a carefully chosen dish and the soil surface covered with moss.

An Ikadabuki style from a yeddo spruce. A six-year-old yeddo spruce, 50cm high; a dish 50 × 35cm, and appropriate tools.

Pull some wire through the mesh covering the drainage holes and use it to secure some pieces of wood to keep the trunk horizontal.

Cut back the tip of the spruce and remove all branches from the side of the trunk to be on the ground. Take out any superfluous branches.

Prune the roots of the tree drastically and wire all the branches to grow upwards. Make 2–3 tongue-shaped cuts on the underside of the trunk to encourage roots to grow quickly. In 2–3 years when you next repot, cut back the old rootball still further to stop it breaking through the soil surface.

Lay the plant in the prepared dish, secure in place and cover the trunk with bonsai soil. Finally lay moss on top and water thoroughly.

77

4 BONSAI TRAINING

The aim of training is to make a good bonsai from your young plant or specimen. In doing this it is usual to look to the centuries-old bonsai tradition of the Japanese for models to emulate. But there is nothing to stop bonsai enthusiasts from going their own way and developing new styles and types that may be latent in the imagination. Nevertheless it is advisable to bear in mind a basic rule of the Japanese masters: the bonsai should look natural, that is to say, you must not lose sight of the tree's growth pattern in the wild. Since a bonsai should be typical of a normal tree, many bonsai growers collect photos or draw sketches of trees or groups of trees to give them ideas for their bonsai. Other sources for ideas include bonsai exhibitions, books on bonsai and bonsai courses which take place regularly in some towns.

Because nature is the model for bonsai shaping it cannot be regarded as an unnatural training such as that found in ornamental styles of hedges and trees—renaissance and baroque, for example. With bonsai training you are not trying to impose an artificial shape on the plants, so you would not, for example, turn straight trees like elms and cypresses into a cascading style when you could use pines and junipers. The miniaturisation of a plant depends on two factors: firstly, the size of the container which acts as a limiting factor on root development and consequently on the intake of food; secondly, the constant pruning back of branches, twigs and roots and the nipping out of shoots and buds. There are also miniature forms of plants in nature, high up in mountains for example, where it is also environmental conditions that cause the limited growth. Even so, these plants look natural and are strong and healthy.

In this chapter we will look at how you can affect the shape of your bonsai. The choice of container for your plant is important, just as much as the pruning and shaping. Wires and other corrective aids offer other ways of influencing the future shape of your bonsai.

This yeddo spruce, *Picea jezoensis*, was found about 50 years ago near Hokkaido and has since been trained as a bonsai. It could be over 150 years old and is 75cm high.

PLANT CONTAINERS

A good bonsai has its roots, trunk, branches and leaves all in proportion. The tree, the surface of the soil with moss or grasses growing on it, and the container are all finely in accord.

Bonsai that grow upright should be placed in shallow, rectangular or oval dishes, whilst weeping trees, as for instance in the cascade style, need to be offset by a deep, round or square dish. The shape of the dish needs to complement the overall form of the plant. A tree with a thick, heavy-looking crown cries out for a weighty container. The colour, too, must be chosen to suit. Trees that flower and those that have light-green leaves go best with light-coloured, glazed dishes. Dark foliage is complemented by shades of dark red, grey or brown. As for size, choose a dish with the width about two-thirds of the height of the tree, if your bonsai is planted on its own. With groups of plants the dish needs to have a width about two-thirds the height of the tallest tree.

To be successful at choosing your container you may find it helpful to develop your sense of taste and feeling for shape by studying acknowledged successes in the art of bonsai.

The bonsai dishes you can buy from specialist dealers usually come from Japan and China and among them you will find a fairly large range of containers in lots of different colours, sizes and shapes. It can be a difficult and time-consuming business finding the right dish, but it is always worth the effort involved.

Glazed dishes

Unglazed dishes

Particularly attractive dishes from Tokoname, Japan, each complete with maker's signature

Antique bonsai dishes from China

PRUNING

This is the most important of the training techniques.

Branch pruning will give you the basic shape of your tree while other methods, such as wiring, help improve upon it.

A well-shaped bonsai needs to have its small branches and twigs cleared away and buds and new shoots removed, a job, therefore, that has to be carried out repeatedly if you are to maintain the shape you have achieved and improve upon it. Tools needed for this are two pairs of sharp scissors, one strong and powerful the other more delicate; and a small saw for thicker branches.

Using special bonsai scissors you will be able to reach every part of your tree and work on it. A little bit of skill is needed for pruning and for style cutting, but patience and a willingness to learn will ensure success. The Table on p. 182 will tell you when and how often to prune, as far as currently available bonsai species are concerned.

Bonsai before and after branch pruning

All branches marked with dotted lines are removed

Branch pruning

Whatever plant you want to train as a bonsai, whether it is something you have found or have bought from a nursery, you must have a mental picture of the shape you want to attain.

Basically, if two branches are growing opposite one another, remove one directly at the trunk; do the same if two are growing forwards, directly above one another or at the same height (*see* branches marked with dotted lines on drawing left). Likewise cut off any lateral branches growing vertically up or down, or crossing the trunk. The cut must be smooth or slightly concave to help the wound to heal.

A thick branch must be cut away with a saw

Make a rough cut first, then saw the remaining stump close to the trunk

Hollow out the cut area with a paring chisel to make the scar neater later on . . .

and seal with grafting wax

If the main shoot of a tree has grown too long, if its tip has broken off, or if you want to retrain your tree, corrective steps can be taken. The example shown here is a *Juniperus squamata meyeri* reduced in height by a third.

A good deciduous bonsai, viewed from above, reveals a finely branching crown with scarcely one branch covering another.

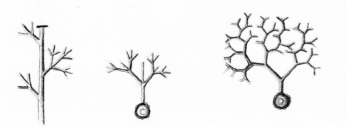

Correctly pruned shoots gradually produce a nicely branching crown.

Pruning of shoots

If you let the new shoots of a bonsai grow unrestrained the crown of the tree would soon race away and become too thick in the upper region. At the same time the inner branches would die because all the growth activity would be concentrated on the tips. So you must continually cut off the new shoots on your tree to reduce the amount by which it increases in height and to distribute the impetus for growth evenly to all branches and sub-branches. How often you cut them back depends on the type of tree, for some only produce new shoots once in the spring while others go on producing throughout the growing period and so must be cut back right through to autumn. The decisive factor regarding how hard you should prune shoots back and where is, of course, the style of tree you wish to create. Shoots should be allowed to grow where you want a new branch to develop. Repeated pruning will produce a nice spread of branches in the crown of the tree, and also produce smaller leaves—both features that will greatly enhance deciduous trees, maples, hornbeams, elms, zelkovas and indoor bonsai. With coniferous trees, too, style trimming techniques will help maintain the tree's shape and encourage smaller needles. All flowering bonsai should only be pruned back after the flowering period.

Detailed information on style trimming techniques for the most important bonsai species will be given in the following chapter.

Black pines, thick-barked black pines, red pines and other 2-needled species: These species of pine have strong, austere-looking tree

Pruning shoots on two-needled pines

shapes and long green needles. For the bonsai-grower they present the apparently difficult task of reducing the size of the needles which are too long in relation to the overall size of a bonsai.

When all of this year's shoots have opened out completely, when summer is reaching its height, take a pair of narrow bonsai scissors and bit by bit cut the shoots away; in contrast to white pines, prune the short shoots first, and a week later the longer ones. This will let all the new shoots grow equally long because you will have given the slower growing shoots an advantage over the faster growing ones. The new shoots which the tree now produces are much shorter than the ones that were removed and they are often more numerous. If several new shoots start to appear where pruning was carried out, only let two shoots continue growing and nip the others in the bud, removing them between thumb and forefinger.

With two-needled pines, using scissors cut away all the needles in autumn to leave only five or six pairs

remove the rest. But if you want your pine to grow thicker leave the three shortest.

Since these candles will grow at different rates, trim back the longest candles repeatedly over the next two or three weeks to keep them in step with the shorter ones (*see* drawings opposite).

If you follow these instructions you should end up with compact, semicircular cushions of needles typical of white pines. With these types of pines and with black pines you should nip out the old needles in autumn to let enough air and light get through to the lower branches.

White pines: These have five needles in each cluster and because they look elegant and have short needles they are very popular for bonsai training. Among white pine saplings the colour of the needles may vary between a bluish tinge and green; the much-prized steel-blue colour is produced in trees that have been grafted. In the spring white pines produce between one and six new shoots, known as candles, at the end of each branch.

Shortly before they open out you should pinch back these candles by one-third or two-thirds, using your fingers. If you think the crown of your tree is thick enough, only keep the two shortest from a cluster of candles and

With all types of pine shorten any overlong branches in autumn

Pruning back of candles on white pines

Branches with one candle

Branches with two candles

Branches with three candles

Pull off old white pine needles in autumn

86

Yeddo spruces, and all other types of spruces: With spruces, when the new shoots are about 2cm long and still soft, they need to be nipped off to about 1cm with a gentle twisting motion of the fingers. This needs to be carried out over a period of about four weeks since the shoots develop at different rates. If your tree is weak only cut back the new shoots on the fairly strong branches. During this period mist spray your tree frequently and stand in a lightly shaded spot.

With fir trees take the shoots back to 1cm when they are still soft

Yews, needle junipers, larches, japanese cedars, cedars: In these trees the buds should be cut back when they start to open out. They will then be about 1–2cm long and should be shortened by half. If you have weak or young trees only cut back the new growth on the strongest branches. Mist spray trees frequently during this time and stand them in a lightly shaded spot.

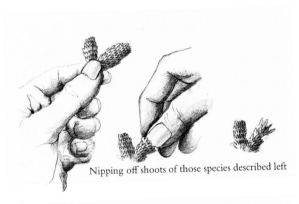

Nipping off shoots of those species described left

Chinese junipers, false cypresses and cypresses: These conifers also produce short shoots that must be continually nipped off between spring and autumn so that only a small piece of the shoot remains (*see* drawing, right). In addition with junipers, remove immediately any shoots growing on thicker branches and directly on the trunk.

Nipping out encourages the plant to grow but should be carried out less and less frequently towards autumn to allow the tree to shut down its growth at the right time before the frosts come.

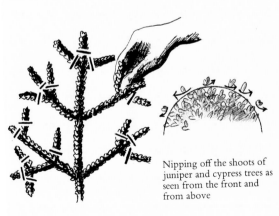

Nipping off the shoots of juniper and cypress trees as seen from the front and from above

Hemlocks: Once only, in early summer reduce new shoots to 1–2cm in length.

Maples, elms, zelkovas, chinese nettle-trees: The shoots of these deciduous trees need to be pruned back from spring through till late summer, younger trees being left with only two or three pairs of leaves. With older trees leave one pair of leaves only and use tweezers to pluck out any shoots that subsequently grow. Two new shoots will develop in the leaf axils and once again only one pair of leaves must be allowed to grow, the tips of the buds being pinched out. These techniques will produce a fine spread of branches at the crown of the tree.

Branches growing very vigorously can be kept in check by removing not only the tips of the shoots but also the leaves of the new shoots at the same time.

Correct pruning for a broom-styled tree

Winter jasmine: Cut shoots back after flowering to one or two leaf pairs. In summer prune back new growth so that two or three pairs of leaves remain, and in early autumn trim long shoots again.

Magnolias: After flowering is finished take the branches back till only two or three leaves remain. In autumn adjust any overlong, non-flowering branches to the same length as the flowering branches.

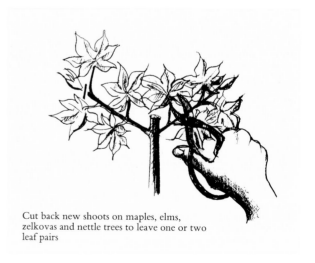

Cut back new shoots on maples, elms, zelkovas and nettle trees to leave one or two leaf pairs

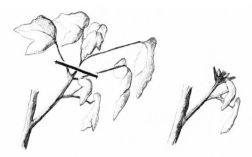

Pruning and simultaneous leaf cutting on vigorous branches

Pricking out of buds on older plants. The earlier these buds are removed the finer the network of branches.

This shows how shoots with overlong gaps between the leaves are cut back. The subsequent new growth produces shorter gaps and smaller leaves.

Pruning of beeches, birches and oaks

grow subsequently can be distinguished as two types: slower growing flowering shoots which will have already put forth buds to blossom the following year and so should not be pruned, and longer shoots which should be trimmed back in summer. Flowering trees often also form suckers on the trunk and these must be removed immediately. Then in autumn all the shoots should be cut back to leave four or five leaf buds.

It is important for the pollination of the flowers to leave the tree somewhere where insects can get at it. If that isn't possible you can pollinate the flowers yourself by dabbing them with ripe stamens.

Birches, oaks, hornbeams, copper beeches and beeches: These deciduous trees develop shoots more slowly and should only ever be pruned back with scissors to leave one or two leaf pairs and then only provided that four or five pairs have already developed.

Apricot, cherry and peach trees: Cut back the flowering branches after the blossom has faded to leave two or three leaf buds, and remove all remaining blossom (unlike apple trees, there is no value in allowing fruits to develop on an apricot tree as they would weaken it). Cutting the branches in this way also maintains the tree's shape. The new shoots that

Pruning of apricot trees; after flowering, shoots are pruned back to leave two or three buds

Apple, pear and other fruit-bearing trees:
After the blossom has faded these trees form new shoots which must be pruned back in summer to two buds. If more shoots appear after pruning they must be removed entirely or pruned back to leave one bud.

To make sure of pollination, pluck off one flower and dab it on the others.

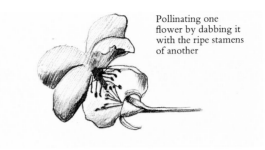

Pollinating one flower by dabbing it with the ripe stamens of another

Azaleas, pomegranates, camellias: These may also be cultivated as indoor bonsai and are described more fully on p. 162ff.

Cotoneasters: New shoots can be cut back repeatedly between spring and late summer to leave two or three leaf buds.

Pruning of a young azalea

Willows: At the beginning of spring before growth restarts prune back the branches to leave two leaf buds; during the growing period cut back the new shoots only if the tree shape demands it.

Hawthorn: Prune new shoots in early summer to 2–3cm long, and repeat in autumn on overlong shoots.

Elaeagnus: Prune back new shoots in late spring to leave two or three leaves and again after a month to leave one or two leaves. Cut off any redundant branches in early autumn or late winter.

With pomegranate trees prune back the shoots after flowering to leave one or two leaf pairs

91

Gardenias: Prune all shoots after the blossom is finished to leave two or three leaf buds, and again after another month to leave two or three leaf pairs. Gardenias may also be kept as indoor bonsai.

Berberis: After four to six pairs of leaves have appeared, continually cut new shoots back to one or two leaf pairs right through to the very end of summer.

Japanese quinces: Repot only in autumn, because if carried out in spring quinces often get attacked by a root disease.

As the same time as repotting, prune all shoots with no flower buds to leave two or three leaf nodules, one or two in older trees. In spring after flowering cut the shoots back to one or two leaf buds. Prune again in autumn to leave four or five buds.

Spindle trees (*Euonymus*): Prune back all shoots to leave two leaf buds either in autumn after the leaves have dropped off or in spring before growth starts. Trim the longest shoots again only at the end of summer.

Forsythias: After flowering shoots have blossomed prune them back to leave one or two pairs of leaves; in mid summer trim new shoots to leave three or four leaf pairs.

Pyracantha: This tree flowers in summer. In spring prune new growth back to leave two or three leaf pairs. Shoots that subsequently grow without flower buds should be cut to the same length as the flowering shoots.

This tree will flower more easily if it is repotted and its roots trimmed every year before growth resumes. Round about mid summer prune back new shoots to leave three or four leaf buds.

Ginkgo: With young ginkgoes let new shoots grow till they have six to eight leaves then prune them back to four or five; with older specimens prune new shoots back to leave one or two leaves.

With young ginkgo trees reduce the new growth to four or five leaves; one or two leaves in older plants

Leaf pruning

Every bonsai grower has to make sure the sizes of the leaves, branches and trunk are in proportion. With small-leaved bonsai the proportions will be right anyway but with other deciduous trees, such as beeches or maples, large leaves can often be obtrusive.

Leaves can be made smaller in various ways. In mid summer, once the leaves have opened out fully, you can remove them with some leaf cutters or a pair of scissors. The tree *must* be strong and healthy, however. The tree will then experience a kind of autumn and shortly afterwards will produce new shoots with leaves, only

When cutting off leaves, if possible leave the stalks on the branch.

With zelkovas the leaves can also be plucked off by hand.

93

this time they will be smaller. If the tree has leaves with long stalks, leave the stalks attached to the branch since it is less injurious to the plant. With short-stalked leaves this is not possible so the leaves should be pinched off directly at the branch.

You can make the process less of a shock for your bonsai if you don't remove all the leaves at once; instead cut off about half to start with, and two weeks later the second half.

Leaf pruning should be carried out in mid summer and not much later, otherwise the new shoots and leaves will mature too late and your tree will be unable to shut down its growth activity sufficiently in advance of the colder weather, thus making it particularly susceptible to frost. Correctly timed leaf pruning also enhances the autumnal colouring.

Leaf pruning is also to be recommended if the crown of the tree has become too thick. Too many leaves keep out too much light and interfere with the circulation of air, particularly as far as the lower branches are concerned. That is why the largest leaves should be pinched out or cut off throughout the summer to stop the crown becoming too dense.

The thickness of a branch can also be affected by pruning its leaves; a branch gets thicker the more leaves it has, and weaker once its leaves have been pruned. Do not add fertiliser to your tree directly before or after leaf pruning. Because less water will be lost through evaporation you'll need to use less when watering. Keep your bonsai in a sheltered spot till new leaf shoots start to appear.

THICKENING THE TRUNK AND BRANCHES

It often happens that the trunk of a bonsai looks too thin in relation to the crown and if this occurs you will have to resolve to thicken it. It is the lower branches that determine the thickness of a tree-trunk, so cut them away only once the trunk is as thick as you want it.

If you want to thicken only the base of the trunk, start in spring by wrapping a piece of aluminium wire round the trunk just below the surface of the soil (*see* drawing below). Above the wire the trunk will swell relatively quickly. Remove the wire in the autumn of the same year otherwise it will constrict the tree too much and it might die.

With a branch that looks too thin you can thicken it up by allowing all its shoots and leaves to grow fully. A branch gets more solid the more foliage it has because its girth increases with the greater amount of nutritive exchange.

Don't worry if a branch left to grow in this way upsets the balance in your bonsai, you can always prune it back later.

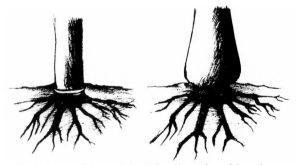

Wind wire round the trunk just below the surface of the soil. The trunk swells very rapidly above this wire ring.

94

This chinese juniper in its antique Chinese bonsai dish is a lovely example of artificial ageing, or jinning as the Japanese call it

ARTIFICIAL AGEING

A tree acquires its beauty and character with age. There are bonsai training methods which enable a tree to look older than it is, and at the same time correct any faults in its shape. The Japanese use three different techniques known as Jin, Sharimiki and Sabamiki.

Jin

The technique of jinning involves leaving branches of the tree that have broken off or died back naturally. Strip away the bark from the branches and sharpen their ends a little if you wish. Smooth along the entire length of the branch with emery paper before painting with citric acid or furniture bleaching agent which in turn bleaches the branch and protects it from rot (*see* drawing below).

Jinning can also be used to make a tree that has grown too tall appear shorter. Simply cut off the leaves or needles at the tip of the tree, remove the bark that is exposed, then proceed as described above. All conifers and some broad-leaves are suitable subjects for jinning.

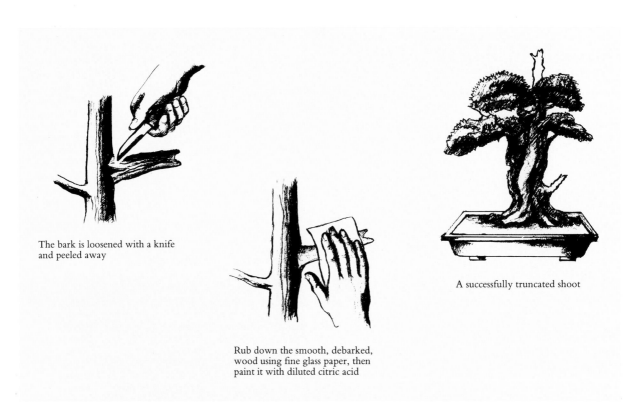

The bark is loosened with a knife and peeled away

Rub down the smooth, debarked, wood using fine glass paper, then paint it with diluted citric acid

A successfully truncated shoot

Sharimiki

The sharimiki method involves partially stripping bark from branches or trunks, and sometimes even from a particularly prominent, visible root. The tree thus gains a more interesting appearance.

Working from the top downwards peel a narrow strip of bark from the front of your tree, having previously loosened the strip by making two vertical incisions with a sharp knife. Use emery paper to smooth the wood down, as for jinning, then apply citric acid or a furniture bleach. Do this carefully so that you make sure the bleach only comes into contact with the areas of the tree stripped of bark.

Sabamiki

Bonsai that have undergone Sabamiki look very old and impressive. They remind you of trees that have withstood the rigours of nature for centuries, particularly those found in highland areas and in solitary coastal sites.

Sabamiki means hollow or split trunk, and it is a wood-splitting technique that enables you to copy the shapes of trees found in nature, particularly among old apricot trees, elaeagnus and junipers. Perhaps you have a bonsai with a damaged trunk, in which case take a chisel and hollow it out at the damaged spot, then treat as you would for jinning and Sharimiki.

Some bonsai experts will also rip out a forward-growing branch that is marring a tree, then using a chisel enlarge the hole left in the trunk. They are then able to train the tree in the Sabamiki style.

All these techniques are best carried out in mid-summer when the wounds will dry quickly and the bleaching agent can soak nicely into the trunk. Always use a sharp knife and smooth the wood down with emery paper before applying the bleach.

Reapply the bleaching agent at least every two years to stop rot attacking the stripped branches and to re-emphasise their light colour.

An example of Sabamiki can be found on page 124, Jin on page 95 and Sharimiki on page 125.

Besides these techniques there is another way of making your tree appear older. Simply tie the branches of your young tree down, or wire them so that their outline more closely resembles those of older trees in the wild.

The age of a tree can only be exactly determined by counting the annual rings
The two fir trunks above show how greatly you can misjudge the age of a tree if you only take into account the thickness of the trunk and not the conditions where it has been growing. These two were collected high in the mountains; one has a diameter of only 3.5cm and 46 annual rings, so is 46 years old, and the other a diameter of 5cm and 96 annual rings, so is 96 years old.

SOIL MIXTURES

The standard mixture is made of equal parts forest soil or peat, loam and coarse, gritty sand. With broadleaves, young trees and vigorously growing trees, a lighter soil is required—one that contains as little loam as possible. Slow-growing bonsai such as pines and the majority of conifers, as well as old trees, do better in a dry soil mixture usually containing more sand. For example, a mixture for broadleaves might consist of one part forest soil, one part peat and one part sand, and a mixture for conifers of two parts sand, one part peat and one part loam.

If garden soil is to be used you should realise that most types already contain some loam. In traditional bonsai training great store is set by the choice of soil and soil mixtures. Every bonsai specialist will swear to the success of his own soil mixtures.

You can of course make the whole matter much simpler for yourself if you fall back on the tried and tested bonsai soils available through retail outlets. They contain one part loam, one part peat and one part granite chippings or coarse grit. The loam content provides the foundation for the mixture, the peat provides the humus so important for the plant, and the coarse grit aids air circulation and drainage, for bonsai want moistness, not wetness.

Of course you can make up this soil mixture for yourself and modify it to suit your bonsai, depending on species. But before you mix any loam, peat and sand, you must first allow the loam and sand to dry then sieve it to remove any dust particles, since dust solidifies the soil and makes the earth less permeable for water and

a Sieved granite chippings can be used as part of the soil mixture and as a drainage layer
b Fresh peat with grit
c Sandy loam

oxygen. Using a sieve with a 0.5mm mesh, throw away all particles that drop through. Bear in mind when mixing your soil that some plants like it very acid (pH 4.5–5.5) and others prefer it less acid (pH 5.8–6). You can buy a meter for measuring pH levels.

To make a soil mixture less acid add lime or calcium carbonate and to reduce the pH level add peat. Azaleas (which prefer acid soils) require less loam and grit and more peat, a good ratio being two parts loam, two parts grit, five parts peat. With broadleaves all will be well with the standard mixture of three parts loam, three parts peat, three parts grit, the proportion of peat being reduced with older trees to check their growth.

Conifers with their predilection for gritty soils will require a higher proportion of grit in the mixture. You can either add grit to the standard earth mixture or make provision for the extra amount when making up your own.

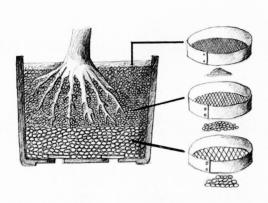

Coarse gravel for drainage, bonsai soil and a wafer-thin covering of loam providing a base for the cushion of moss. All the ingredients should be sieved first to remove dust.

High time to repot!

WIRING TECHNIQUES AND OTHER TRAINING METHODS

Should you want to alter the direction in which your bonsai's branches are growing or to shape its trunk, there are various techniques you might like to employ.

One of them is the rather difficult technique of wiring. It is used if you want to make a bonsai look older, for example, by means of low-hanging branches, or if you want to keep a bend in the trunk or want one eliminated. Use malleable copper or anodised aluminium wire which is available in different thicknesses from specialist trade outlets.

Information on what time of year to carry out wiring for particular species is given on p. 182.

In the main it is conifers that are wired, for with broadleaves the desired shape can usually be arrived at by pruning alone. Nevertheless if you still want to wire broadleaves do so in spring when the tree is full of sap, and remove the wire again after six to eight months at the latest. Evergreen trees and conifers take longer for their shapes to change. However, even with these trees, the wire should be taken off after twelve to eighteen months at the latest, and certainly before it begins to cut into the bark. But if the situation has gone beyond this point, making it impossible to remove the wire without greatly damaging the bark, let it stay in the trunk or branch and use wire cutters to remove it from the areas that have not been cut into. Always wire a bonsai in the direction of growth, that is, by coiling the wire round in a spiral working from the bottom upwards, and use one or two wires depending on how thick the trunk

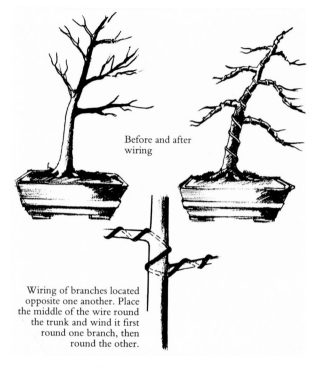

Before and after wiring

Wiring of branches located opposite one another. Place the middle of the wire round the trunk and wind it first round one branch, then round the other.

or branch is. Repeat the wiring as often as is necessary to achieve the shape you want. Do make sure you don't trap any leaves or needles under the wire coils. Choose a wire barely a third as thick as the diameter of the branch you want to wire (using the point at which it is thickest as a measure). Another rule of thumb states that the thinnest wire that will hold a branch in the required shape is the right one. If it is the trunk that is to be wired secure the end of the wire at the back of the trunk by pushing it into the earth right down to the bottom of the dish. Then wind the wire in a spiral round the trunk, each coil making an angle of about 45° with the line of the trunk. Keep the distance between the coils even, only letting it get smaller nearer the top. Instead of one thick wire you could use two thinner ones held close together. The coils should be neither too loose nor too tight. The same technique is used for branch wiring, only in this case the wire is secured to the trunk or to an opposite branch. Carefully bend the wired area to the required shape.

Small branches growing down must be removed before wiring

too close   too far apart   correct

Correctly wired using wires of different thicknesses

After wiring a branch or trunk bend it carefully in the desired direction

101

Wire stays change the direction in which the trunk is growing.

There are other ways of making branches bend down:

1 Fix wires to the plant container and then attach the branches to them one by one.
2 Attach wire to the trunk and tie the branches to it.
3 Use lead weights or small plastic bags filled with sand to weigh the branches down.

It is important to pad the areas to which the wire on the branch is attached, to prevent the bark being damaged. You can use a piece of rubber for this, perhaps the sort used for a bicycle inner tube.

If some of your branches are too close to one another you can bend them apart with the aid of a bit of wood, and if there is too much of a gap between two trunks or branches you can use a wire to bring them closer together again.

You can give a trunk some nice curves, or indeed remove some, by placing wire or metal rods parallel to the trunk and fixing them in place with raffia. A small screw-clamp will often be useful for this. If the tree is damaged by the wire the wounds must be sealed with grafting wax.

After training techniques such as wiring your bonsai will need to be allowed to recover. Never wire a bonsai and repot it at the same time. After wiring leave the tree in a protected spot for a few weeks.

Fix wires on to the plant container and tie the branches to it with string

Bending a branch down using a stone weight

Branch and trunk tied together with wire or string secured to the trunk

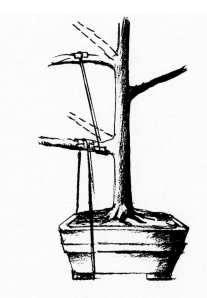

Another method of bending branches in a required direction

A piece of wood bending two branches apart

Branch tied to the trunk

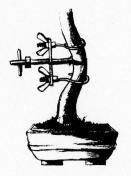

A screw-clamp being used to give a well-defined curve to a trunk

A strong piece of wire or metal rod fixed parallel to the trunk to give a bend, or to eliminate one

BUYING BONSAI

If you want to be spared the trouble of cultivating your own bonsai you can buy ready-trained specimens; there is a large selection but beware of widely differing quality. Nearly all of them come from Japan and China. They range from young trees that have only undergone the first steps of training, through those whose training is half complete to masterpieces of the bonsai art. Conifers, evergreens, broadleaves and flowering species are all equally well represented.

In recent times bonsai have always been imported with soil attached and usually growing in a container. Nevertheless, when you buy one, always test that the bonsai is well rooted. A firm, compact surface of soil and an unbroken layer of moss will lead you to believe that the tree has been planted for a fairly long time, although it might have been repotted recently. A healthy bonsai should also look like a nice, strong, small tree, its foliage as intensely coloured as the species and season dictates.

Don't be influenced by the age given for the tree, it is much more important for its value that it has a natural shape. The pictures on the right show a small selection of good value bonsai.

Chinese juniper *Juniperus chinensis*, height about 40cm, age about 15 years

a) *Zelkova serrata* about 10 years
b) *Pinus parviflora* about 12 years
c) *Juniperus chinensis* about 8 years
d) *Juniperus chinensis* about 15 years

Zelkova *Zelkova serrata*, height about 15cm, age about 8 years

Apricot *Prunus mume*, height about 40cm, age about 15 years

Japanese red maple *Acer palmatum* 'Atropurpureum'
height about 40cm, age about 10 years

Paradise apple *Malus pumila*, height about 30cm, age about 12 years

HALLMARKS OF A GOOD BONSAI

The visible roots of a bonsai should grow in every direction. They need not be of the same thickness nor be the same distance apart, but they must never cross over.

The transition from root to trunk should be clearly visible. A good bonsai gives the impression that its trunk is firm and secure, well rooted in the soil.

The shape and appearance of the trunk is of particular importance in miniature trees. It is usually visible from the roots to high up in the crown of the tree, and should taper away towards the top. That is why special care and attention is given to getting its shape right. The trunk can be straight or bent. The older it appears to be, the more value is placed on the tree. Curves and bends in the trunk and branches should look natural; bizarre and grotesque shapes just look artificial. A bonsai, moreover, has a front and back, the front being the side on which as much as possible of the structure of the trunk and branches is to be seen. For this reason branches never grow forwards in a bonsai, always to the sides or to the rear. It is only in the top part of the crown that small branches and twigs are allowed to grow out to the front, for artistic reasons. The only exception is the broom style.

A bonsai has relatively few branches and it is almost impossible to avoid removing branches; these will leave behind visible cuts to start with. It is not true that the bonsai loses a good part of its value by being pruned, so long, that is, as the cuts are made expertly enough to leave the scars virtually undetectable a couple of years later.

This tree has all the qualities of a good bonsai, a strong trunk tapering towards the top and correctly trained branches

All branches are trained very carefully. Let's call the main branch No. 1 and say it grows to the left, then No. 2 might perhaps grow towards the back and No. 3 towards the right. No two branches should be at the same height, an aspect that can easily be checked by looking down on your tree from above. No branch should completely hide another or grow parallel to another. With a bent trunk the branches should always be located on the outer curve. They should get smaller towards the tip and taper at the end.

The leaves on a good bonsai are as small as possible, so that the proportions between trunk, branches and leaves hold true; they should also have a strong, healthy colour.

Needle juniper
Juniperus rigida,
informal upright style—
Moyogi
height about 70cm,
over 200 years old

Japanese red maple, *Acer palmatum dissectum* 'Atropurpureum', informal upright style—Moyogi, height 45cm, age about 40 years, in spring

The same tree in its autumn colours

Crab apple
Malus halliana
mame bonsai
height 15cm
age about 10 years

Close-up
of the same tree

Chinese japonica *Chaenomeles chinensis*, height 48cm, age about 65 years, informal upright style—Moyogi

Apricot *Prunus mume*, literati—Bunjingi, height about 60cm, age about 50 years

Japanese red maple *Acer palmatum dissectum* 'Atropurpureum' clinging-to-rock style—Ishitsuki, height 38cm, age about 16 years

Zelkova *Zelkova serrata*, broom style—Hokidachi, height 45cm, age about 50 years, from the author's collection

Trident maple
Acer buergeriamum,
growing in an antique
Chinese dish.
About 35 years old,
this tree is a particularly fine
specimen from the author's
bonsai collection.

Detail of trunk of
the trident maple opposite

Chinese elm
Ulmus parviflora,
height about 45cm,
age about 45 years,
presented to the author by
the Shanghai tree nursery.
Traditional animal shapes
are still popular in Chinese
bonsai training even today.

(opposite) Japanese maple *Acer palmatum* clump—Kabudachi, height about 85cm, age about 70 years

Japanese white pine, *Pinus parviflora*. This bonsai is made up of three styles—semi-cascade, clump and windswept. Height about 70cm, age about 85 years.

Japanese apricot
Prunus mume,
literati style—Bunjingi,
height about 55cm,
over 120 years old

(oppo
Serissa foe
in China know
'tree of a thousand st
height about 50
age about 35 ye

This Japanese white pine,
Pinus parviflora,
height 94cm,
is over 150 years old.
It certainly looks a very
weathered tree.

Chinese juniper,
Juniperus chinensis,
height about 77cm,
age about 180 years

5 GENERAL CARE OF BONSAI

Good bonsai are valuable and rare. Some are, like works of art, irreplaceable. Appropriate care is very important for a bonsai, and includes repotting at the right time, the correct soil mixture and, most importantly, correct watering. Other considerations are feeding, choosing the right site, overwintering and taking precautions against disease.

If you have any questions about caring for your bonsai or if problems arise, get in touch with a bonsai expert who may be able to help with his knowledge and experience. A good specialist bonsai centre should also have facilities for taking in plants over the holidays or for keeping them over the winter, as well as for nursing sick plants back to health. In such cases being a member of, or having contact with, a good bonsai club can be very helpful, for information and the sharing of experience usually lie at the heart of the club's activities.

ROOT PRUNING

Roots should be pruned whenever a plant is potted for the first time and every time it is repotted. In young trees they should be cut by about one third; in very old bonsai the whole root ball should be reduced by about 2–3cm all round.

The older a plant is, the less of the root mass should be cut away, for older trees produce

(opposite)
A fine image to be captured as a bonsai. Linden tree in the castle grounds, Heidelberg, Germany.

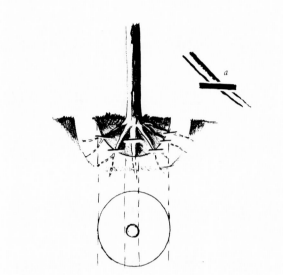

Make sure when root pruning that the inner root area stays intact. With thicker roots the cut edge should always point downwards (a).

fewer shoots and correspondingly fewer roots. Make sure when you prune your roots that the inner root area remains intact. With bigger roots the cut area should always point downwards.

POTTING AND REPOTTING

Every two years a young tree needs a 1–2cm bigger pot. The first time a bonsai is planted in a dish it is called potting up; whenever it is transferred to a bigger pot it is called potting on. An older specimen should be repotted when the soil is exhausted and needs changing or when the roots have grown so dense that they need pruning. In this case the tree can be repotted in the same dish. How often the soil and container should be changed will depend on the species, age and condition of the plant. Fast-growing broadleaves need repotting about once every two years, conifers about once every two to five years. The Table on page 182 will tell you what time of year to transplant your bonsai and also gives some suggestions on how often to transplant young and middle-aged trees.

A bonsai often remains in the same container for years, which is why the correct soil composition is so important.

Just before repotting allow your bonsai to dry out a bit more than usual to make it easier to remove the soil from the root ball. Lift the plant out carefully from the dish. Now remove about half the old earth from the root ball using a pointed stick and being careful not to damage the fine fibrous roots.

Any roots that are too thick, damaged or dead should be cut away and the entire root system pruned back by about a third. With thicker roots the cut area should always point downwards.

Cover the drainage holes of the dish with a piece of plastic mesh to stop the soil trickling out. Pull plastic-coated wire or aluminium wire—not copper—through the drainage holes to fix the root ball or plant in position. This is especially recommended for large trees and for any that are going to be put in very shallow dishes, as you don't want the wind to blow the trees over. Remove the wire six months later by which time new roots will have formed. Cover the bottom of the dish with a layer of coarse gravel (no deeper than 2cm) to aid drainage. On

top of that comes a layer of the actual planting soil. It should be nearly dry so that it trickles nicely and fills the spaces between the roots.

Now place the bonsai in the dish, spreading the roots on all sides. The visible roots should lie roughly at the height of the edge of the dish or a little above it. Next fix the tree in place with the wire that you have pushed through. Always press the earth down firmly as you fill the dish, particularly at the edges. Use a small piece of wood for this or your thumb. To stop gaps forming in the soil tap the edge of the dish frequently with your knuckles. The surface of the earth should look like an expanse of countryside, so with any bonsai the soil level should be no more than 0.5cm below the rim of the dish. Please don't just plonk your tree in the middle of the dish, but decide on a spot where you think it will be seen to best advantage. The Japanese have devised strict rules regarding this, (*see* p. 180).

A fine layer of loam sieved on top of the soil stops it seeping out when the plant is watered and also helps new moss to grow again more quickly. Finally, brush the surface smooth and water the tree thoroughly. After repotting a bonsai it must be put in a semi-shaded spot protected from the wind, before being returned to its normal site two or three weeks later. A month later at the earliest, once new roots have formed, the bonsai can be given fertiliser again for the first time.

Carefully remove the tree from its container

Using a wooden stick remove about half the old earth from the root ball

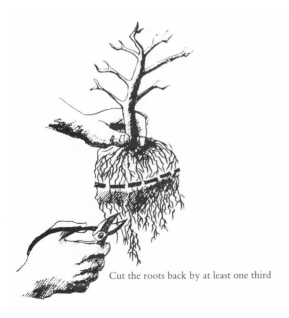

Cut the roots back by at least one third

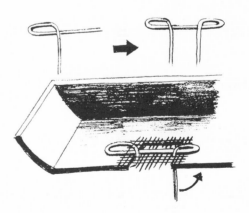

Use a loop of wire like this to secure the mesh over the drainage hole in the dish.

To secure the root ball in position a wire can be pulled through the drainage holes, before a coarse gravel layer about 2cm deep is tipped in

Adding bonsai soil on top of the drainage layer

Placing the tree in the dish and securing with wire

Topping the dish up with bonsai soil to just below the rim.

Press earth down firmly particularly at the edge.

Sieve a fine layer of loam on top before brushing soil smooth.

Water the tree thoroughly and stand it in a protected spot.

Cross-section of bonsai dish

131

MOSS AND OTHER GROUND COVER

Moss gives the impression of a velvety forest carpet and is particularly effective where trees have visible roots. It not only looks good, but also stops soil seeping out when the bonsai is wanted. You can break up a blanket of moss by interspersing club moss (*Selaginella*), *Acorus*, wild cyclamen (*Cyclamen persicum*) and low-growing species of *Crassulacea*.

Please remember that a thick covering of moss on top of the soil means that moisture may be retained that much longer, so you might need to water less frequently. Similarly, moss must not be allowed to grow high up the trunk because rot might set in.

The prettiest moss develops of its own accord in the open air after about six to eight months, provided enough moisture is present. If you don't want to wait that long you can place pieces of moss on top instead. Moss can be found in damp places, in the corners of roofs, in cracks in the walls, between paving-stones and on rocks. Moss found growing in woods is not a good idea because it grows too tall. Many bonsai growers let the moss that they have gathered dry, then rub it and sow the crumbs on the soil.

Birds, particularly blackbirds and sparrows, can be a source of great annoyance to the bonsai enthusiast because they tend to scratch away the best covering of moss in their search for food. To deter them you can temporarily fix tinfoil to the tree.

The beauty moss can bring to bonsai. The light-coloured plants in the foreground are club-mosses, *Selaginella*.

132

A 55 year old Sageretia
Sageretia theesans
from China, with an
attractive carpet of
moss displayed in
an antique bonsai dish,
height about 45cm

WATERING

Like all plants bonsai need sufficient water, but too much water can be very harmful. If the earth is kept too wet the roots begin to rot because the circulation of air is impeded. All bonsai dishes do, however, have large enough drainage holes in the bottom to enable the excess water to flow quickly away. A good soil mixture with its granular consistency will also help make sure that any excess water is not retained too long.

A greater danger lies, however, in drying out, particularly in summer, on account of the small amount of root available to miniature trees. You must ensure that a bonsai's soil is always kept slightly damp—all year round. If, despite your vigilance, the soil does get very dry, stand the plant in water up to the edge of its dish for about ten minutes so that it can suck up all it wants.

Individual plants have their own requirements which are worth investigating. (Compare instructions given in the Table on p. 182.) Some species will want to be kept drier, and others moister. Temperature, humidity and season are other factors that need to be taken into consideration. In summer bonsai often have to be watered several times daily, in winter (the resting period) less often, perhaps only once a week. Water your bonsai less if it is sick, for then its root system is normally less efficient and cannot take up as much water. If your tree uses less water and stays moist for longer than usual it is a sure sign that its roots have been damaged. It also needs less water during the first three to four weeks after its roots or leaves have been pruned, for in the first case fewer roots can cope only with a smaller amount of water, and in the

The author with his bonsai collection. Spraying from above removes dust from the leaves and branches, but should be avoided in the midday heat of the summer sun to stop the leaves from burning.

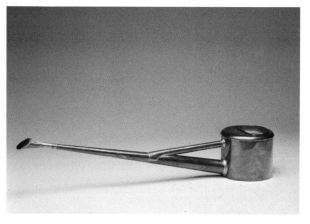

A beautiful but practical Japanese bonsai watering-can made of copper. The neck of the can is precisely gauged for producing the necessary pressure to get the water through the very fine nozzle.

second case the area of evaporation has been reduced by removing the leaves.

It is quite important to be more sparing with your watering in the spring when your tree is getting its new shoots and leaves. This will stop the leaf interval along the new shoots being too great and prevent the leaves from getting too big.

Soft water is best for watering. Very hard water should be softened with decalcifying tablets (available from aquarists or pet shops). It is also possible to collect rain water. With tap water let it stand for two or three days so that any traces of chlorine are precipitated out. Water that has been left standing has also the advantage of being lukewarm. Spray the tree from above several times in succession using a very fine spray watering-can. This is necessary because, so as not to disturb the harmony between dish and tree, bonsai have only a very small space between the soil and the top of the dish, and so can only accept a little water at a time. Repeat the spraying until the entire root ball has absorbed sufficient water. In mid-summer, to avoid burning the leaves, don't spray your tree at midday when it is hottest, leave it till late afternoon or do it in the morning. A rain shower is good news for your bonsai but a week of uninterrupted rain is not well tolerated by most species. The rain water remains too long in the dishes because it cannot flow away quickly enough through the drainage holes and the young roots start to rot. The same thing happens if you stand your bonsai dish on a saucer; after a thorough watering the tree will literally be standing in water.

During an uninterrupted period of rain tilt the bonsai to let the water run away

I can suggest two ways of avoiding this problem (*see* drawing above). Either tilt your bonsai so that the water can run off more quickly, or rig up a collar made of plastic film or strong cardboard and lay it at an angle on the surface of the soil so that the rain can run off and not soak into the soil. If you are going to be away from home for any length of time, a holiday perhaps, you must find someone who can be relied upon to care for your bonsai properly. A friend who has bonsai of his or her own, or a garden centre/nursery where they are familiar with bonsai are probably your best bet.

FEEDING

As any plant grows it extracts various elements from the soil. In addition, large amounts of elements are washed away through repeated watering and these have to be replaced if the plant is to continue to grow strong and healthy. This is particularly important with bonsai, because unlike garden plants they have to obtain these necessary substances from a very limited soil area. For the same reason over-feeding often produces an effect opposite to the one a bonsai grower wants. The plant produces shoots that are too long, leaves that are too big and branches that are too thick. It is important to realise that a tree doesn't die back from a lack of fertiliser but rather from too much, for the roots can be damaged and in the worst cases the tree may actually die.

If your bonsai looks poorly, first ascertain whether this is due to a lack of fertiliser or to root damage. Lift the tree out of the dish and check whether it has new, white tips to its roots. If it has, this is a sign that the root system is healthy and would accept fertiliser, currently lacking. However, if the tips of the roots are brown and squashed and easy to pull off, they are dead and will not be able to take more fertiliser.

How much feed to add and when to give it depends on the requirements of the individual plants. As a rule young trees need more nutrients than old ones; fast-growing trees more than slower-growing ones. Hardwoods are given fertiliser after the first shoots appear and until they begin to shed their leaves; softwoods until mid-autumn at the latest. Do not feed any plants during winter, the resting period. Flowering plants must not be fed immediately before or during the flowering period because it will make them shed their blossom early, and growth will be concentrated on the shoots. Instead, wait till early summer when the fruit has begun to form. At the same time phosphorus can be added to enhance the blossom, ensuring that the following spring your tree will flower that bit more luxuriantly.

Stop feeding immediately after repotting as the root system is weakened by root pruning. Plants with ailing roots are also unable to absorb nutrients; they should be fed as little as you would feed in the hottest period of summer when trees generally suspend growth for a short time and so don't require additional nutrients. As a rule pure organic fertilisers are used in preference to inorganic ones since these may cause burning damage to the roots on account of their salt content if they are not properly applied. Well-known organic fertilisers are bone-meal, horn and hoof meal, fish-meal and rape-seed, all of which are available individually or as mixtures. Simply spread them evenly over the surface of the earth, roughly 1 tsp/100m² of soil. Organic fertilisers take effect more slowly because the active agents in them are released into the soil only gradually, only then becoming accessible to the plant; inorganic fertilisers, on the other hand, particularly liquid ones, can be absorbed immediately by the roots—a property which is useful when your plant is in urgent need.

If using any of the commonly available liquid fertilisers follow the instructions given for pot plants as regards the concentration to apply. Don't forget to water your bonsai thoroughly before feeding.

Japanese bonsai growers use pelletised organic fertiliser. It consists of rape seed, bone and fish meal combined together in an ideal ratio for bonsai, and is very easy to use. The fertiliser pellets are laid on top of the soil roughly in the middle between the trunk and the edge of the dish. For small dishes measuring approximately 15×10cm you will need about one pellet, for medium-sized dishes (15×20cm) about two pellets, and for large dishes (30×40cm) about four pellets. During watering, the pellets slowly break up; should they become exhausted, new pellets need only be applied in their place until towards the end of the summer because they remain effective for so long.

As mentioned earlier, all the fertilisers you can buy contain the most important nutrients in the correct proportions as far as the majority of plants are concerned. They often differ, however, in the ratio of the individual ingredients in a mixture. Your choice can be made easier if you have an exact knowledge of the special needs of your tree and if you understand the effect of the most important nutrients and trace elements on plants in general. You can alter the pH value of the soil simply by applying extra amounts and you can have a marked effect on the way your plants will grow.

Rubber tree, *Ficus retusa*, indoor bonsai
height 32cm
age about 20 years

Nitrogen

This element controls the growth of the leaves and shoots in a plant. Too much nitrogen is harmful, for the plant develops large, very dark green leaves and delays the production of blossom and the maturation of the wood. Plants are also more susceptible to disease. Nitrogen deficiency is suggested by the pale colour and poor growth of the leaves. Nitrogen is usually present in sufficient quantity in fertilisers. Otherwise it can also be added as calcium nitrate or, in the case of plants that are particularly acid-loving, as potassium nitrate.

Phosphorus

This encourages the growth of roots and flowers. Unlike nitrogen a plant will not take up more phosphorus than it needs. A lack of it is indicated by a reddish tinge to the leaves which also point upwards. Superphosphate applied at the beginning of summer for about two months, in the correct quantities for bonsai, will improve the blossom.

Potash

This helps in the maturing of the wood and increases the absorptive capacity of the roots; it makes the plants more robust overall. A lack of potash is evident from brownish flecks and curling edges on the leaves. I would suggest a proprietary potash which also contains the important ingredient magnesium, or else sulphate of potash can be used.

Calcium

This controls the absorption of phosphorous and potash and affects the growth of roots. A lack of lime causes the vegetative points to die back. Soil test kits are available to test the pH level, and if this is low carbonate of lime can be applied to rectify things.

Over-fertilising with lime causes a yellow tinge to appear on the leaves (lime chlorosis), for lime prevents the plant from absorbing iron from the soil, (*see* Iron, below).

Iron

Among the trace elements such as magnesium, iron, sulphur, manganese, boron, copper, zinc, molybdenum and others, most of which are catalysers in plant metabolism, iron is of particular importance. It is responsible for the development of chlorophyll, thus a lack of iron produces chlorosis of the leaves. This can be rectified by watering the plant with a solution of chelated or sequestered iron.

Japanese red maple, *Acer palmatum* 'Atropurpureum', displayed in a dish measuring 40cm × 28cm complete with fertiliser pellets.

Bonsai nursery belonging to the Takeyama family, Omiya, Japan

SITING YOUR BONSAI

The conventional bonsai requires a site in the open air. In the garden, on an open balcony, on a patio or roof garden your tree is exposed to the atmospheric conditions—sun, wind and rain—that it needs to remain healthy and develop satisfactorily.

A bonsai may be brought into the house as a decoration only for a few hours a week, a day at the most. Outside, keep your plants raised off the ground as it makes them easier to tend and admire and less at risk from pests or even pets.

The ideal site for your bonsai is a shelf or framework that can be shaded in the summer if necessary and roofed over with a plastic covering in winter. The majority of bonsai species require full sunlight. Only a few sensitive plant species have to be kept slightly shaded (*see* Table, p. 182).

If the sunlight falls on one side only, you must turn your bonsai every few weeks to stop it developing in an unbalanced way.

You can make up for any lack of sunshine—for example, if a balcony is overhung by a roof—by applying artificial light. Natural, or daylight, fluorescent lamps can be used for this purpose.

Bonsai growers who don't have a balcony can stand their trees on a wide window-sill and secure them with elastic or wire.

Even on a balcony your trees must be made safe against storms.

A framework like this makes
an ideal site for your bonsai.
It is shaded in summer and
can be roofed over with
plastic sheeting in winter.

A display room in Heidelberg's bonsai centre.

142

Japanese beech forest *Fagus crenata*, height about 60cm, age about 6–25 years, displayed on a flat piece of stone

OVERWINTERING

There should be no problem with overwintering if you keep all bonsai at temperatures of between 0°C and +5°C. A greenhouse is ideal because it is bright and relatively humid. But as not everyone has access to a greenhouse some other ways of overwintering your bonsai need to be suggested.

Hardy species

For species such as pines, junipers and beeches, (*see* Table, p. 182), you can construct a plastic cover small enough to go on a balcony if that's the only space you have. Take a box and fill it with a moist mixture of peat and sand or Perlite, then sink your trees into it to cover the edge of the bonsai dishes. (Ceramic dishes will be protected from any frost damage by doing this.) To make a roof bend some steel or bamboo rods and stick them in the corners of the box. Then cover this framework with a sheet of plastic and tuck the ends under the box. If the weather is mild and the sun is shining the plastic sheet should be rolled up to let some air get in. This is very important so as not to expose your bonsai to too much of a variation in temperature. If you want to avoid having to ventilate your chamber use a perforated opalescent plastic, rather than a clear one, or stand it in the shade.

Another possibility for overwintering your bonsai is a porous block of polystyrene or Oasis with holes cut in that you can place the dishes in. Use double-strength PVC sheets stuck together as a wind-break.

Any bonsai to be left outside in winter should not be brought indoors as a decoration after the end of the summer so that they can harden off before the frosts come.

In winter sink your bonsai in some damp peat so that it reaches over the rim of your dishes. Make sure your box has drainage holes to stop water building up.

After sinking your plants in the peat brace bamboo, willow or steel rods against the corners of your box. Now cover this framework with perforated opalescent plastic, tucking the ends under the box.

Half-hardy species

Trident maple and cypresses, for example (*see* Table, p. 182), can tolerate temperatures that drop to −5°C. You have a choice with these species: either install a heat lamp in your self-constructed shelter or keep the plants with frost-sensitive species.

Frost-sensitive species

Keep boxwoods, myrtles and serissas in un-heated, bright rooms, in hallways, in well-lit store cupboards or in conservatories.

Please ensure that wherever you keep your bonsai the temperature never rises above +8°C, otherwise the trees will wake from their winter slumber and start to produce shoots. And don't forget either to spray your plants frequently, perhaps twice a week, to keep the air sufficiently humid. Any plants kept in the open air or under a plastic covering during the winter should not be sprayed.

Entrance to a cellar that can be covered over with plastic sheeting, as used by Rolf and Gisela Kunitsch of Altheim for overwintering their bonsai. A cellar window that catches a bright shaft of light is also a good place during the winter.

BONSAI TOOLS

In the early stages of cultivating bonsai it is possible to make do with equipment you are likely to have to hand, secateurs and pruning shears, for example. In the long run, however, you won't be able to do without tools specially designed for bonsai. Slender bonsai scissors, for instance, make it possible to reach every branch and root on your plants. Pliers for removing wire are so designed that they won't damage the bark, and the pliers used for making a concave incision leave behind a wound that heals quickly, without nasty scarring.

The bonsai tools pictured here, developed in Japan, are the most important ones you'll need. Provided you treat them carefully, in particular giving them a thorough clean after use, they should last a long time and give good service.

These long, slender bonsai scissors are specially designed to enable you to reach all the small branches within the thick crown of a tree

Leaf cutters for nipping off young shoots and leaves

Larger bonsai scissors for cutting thicker branches and roots

146

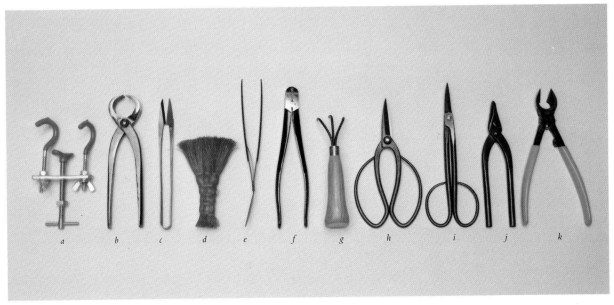

a   Screw-clamp for bending branches and trunks
b   Pliers for cutting thick roots
c   Leaf cutters
d   Brush for cleaning and smoothing the surface of the soil
e   Tweezers for pinching out young shoots, removing wilted leaves
      and aphids
f   Wire cutters for removing wire
g   Rake for separating out matted roots when repotting
h   Scissors for cutting shoots, branches and thinnish roots
i   Scissors for cutting fine shoots and thinning out twigs in the
      crown of a tree
j   Pliers for unwinding wire on wired trees, also suitable as a
      jinning tool
k + l Concave-cutting pliers for cutting branches off very close to the
      trunk, a very important bonsai tool
m   Saw for sawing off thick branches
n   Paring or wood chisel for gouging out a fairly large incision
o   Anodised aluminium wire in various thicknesses

The wire cutters are specially designed for nipping through the wire on the tree without damaging the bark.

Branch cutters enable you to cut even fairly thick branches directly at the trunk. A concave incision helps the cut heal more quickly and neatly than with conventional scissors.

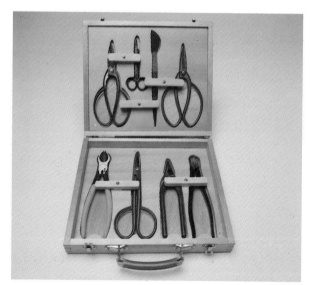

A slender, practical wooden case containing eight of the most important bonsai tools.

A Japanese white pine collected in the mountains, here standing on a turntable that can be adjusted upwards by some 40cm. The shelf on the right is for tools. The 2 drawers can be used for housing the tools when not in use.

Japanese azalea *Azalea japonica*
informal upright form—Moyogi,
height about 65cm, age about 100 years,
displayed in an antique Chinese bonsai dish
whose colour and shape complement
so superbly this truly lovely azalea

PESTS AND DISEASES

The best way of protecting your bonsai against disease is to look after it carefully and to check it over regularly. But if you ever do have occasion to tackle diseases, pests, fungi and such-like, they will be the same sort of things that also attack house and garden plants. If the cause of a disease cannot be traced back to incorrect care of the plant or to the leaf area, the first thing to do is to lift the plant carefully out of its container. Strong, white tips to the roots usually mean that the root system is functioning all right and so the disease symptoms haven't started from there.

There are several commercially available treatments for disease, any of which you can use, following the dosages given in the manufacturers' instructions. Never use a stronger dose than directed. As a preventive measure against diseases and harmful insects it is a good idea to spray all bonsai every spring just before growth restarts. Use one of the special 'spring insecticides' and to combat fungi spray in addition with a proprietary fungicide.

In the following few pages we will look at the most important diseases and pests which can attack bonsai. Whenever you have any problems with your bonsai turn to an expert for advice and make regular and frequent visits to your specialist bonsai centre—better once too often than once too late.

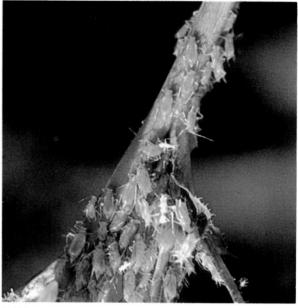
Aphids

Pests

Aphids: These are usually found on the undersides of leaves and on buds. It is often possible simply to wash them off with a strong jet of water, or else a light spray with a suitable insecticide will eliminate them.

Caterpillars

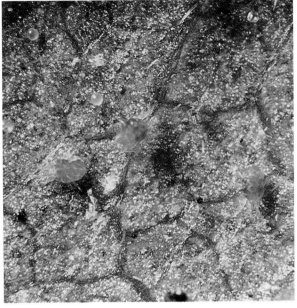

Red spider mites

Caterpillars: These are easily traced because they leave behind obvious signs of the leaves having been eaten. If you can't find them and simply pick them off the plant, it will have to be sprayed with a Metasystox solution or other insecticide.

Red spider mites: These crop up particularly on junipers, black pines, firs and zelkovas when the conditions are drier than usual. They make the needles and leaves look yellow or pale. Usually only parts of a plant are affected. You'll be able to see the mites by holding a sheet of white paper under an affected branch and tapping it. They look like paprika powder and are easily identifiable under a microscope. Special treatments are needed to combat the red spider mite: when the vegetative period begins use a proprietary insecticide and follow the manufacturer's instructions.

Ants: These are pests only insofar as they appear in conjunction with aphids. You must, therefore, keep the area surrounding your bonsai free of ants. There are many antkillers on the market.

Malaysian bark beetle: This occurs only infrequently but is very difficult to keep under control. It is a 3cm-long black beetle with white spots and long black-and-white striped antennae. It hatches at the end of spring and starts eating away the bark in rings, and in so doing may debark whole branches, perhaps killing the tree. Its eggs are laid among the branches, the white larvae that hatch from them eating their way through into the trunk where they pupate. Their presence is evident from gall-like swellings on the trunk. Another clue to their presence is circular holes in the trunk and branches. After a fairly lengthy resting period the larvae once again turn into beetles, then the cycle begins again. An infestation should be treated by removing affected branches and by spraying with Malathion every three weeks.

Earthworms: These are not in themselves harmful, but their tunnelling affects drainage and so they should be removed.

Snails: These will eat the trees. They also leave behind unsightly mucous trails. Either pick the snails off early in the mornings or put down small quantities of slug pellets on the surface of the soil to get rid of them.

White worms: These thread-like worms, 0.5cm in length and white in colour, often crop up when organic fertilisers are used. They are harmless and can be eliminated with a weak solution of Metasystox.

Scale insects

Scale insects: These colonise twigs and the undersides of leaves in both soft and hardwood trees appearing as brown, pock-like swellings. In many cases they can simply be removed with your hand. If the attack is a severe one use an insecticide or you can spray your tree several times with a 0.15% Malathion-emulsion.

Woolly aphids

Root aphids

Woolly aphids: These may be found on the trunk, in the fork of a branch or at the junction between branches and leaves. They look like tiny balls of cotton wool and can be treated in the same way as aphids after first prising apart the woolly balls with a stick.

Root aphids: Whilst they are growing, these aphids cause the leaves of a tree to wilt. They are white insects that inhabit tree roots, but must not be confused with the white mould found in pine trees that clings together in a crinkly ball and smells of fungus. This is in fact a beneficial fungus (*Mycorrhiza*) that lives symbiotically with pines, its presence signifying that all is well.

Root aphids can be eliminated with an insect-icide sprayed directly onto the roots. An alternative is a solution of Metasystox.

Chlorosis

True mildew

Diseases

Chlorosis or jaundice: Leaves and needles turn yellow whilst the leaf veins stay green, the chief cause being a lack of iron. Treat by watering your plant with sequestered iron.

Soil that is too dense and wet can produce the same results, as the plant is unable to get enough oxygen. In this case it helps to break up the soil, even repot the plant if necessary, and water a bit less.

True mildew: This is identifiable as a white, floury coating on the upper sides of leaves. It occurs when temperatures are high combined with a lack of air circulation or the humidity being too high. Mildew is a fungal disease and so is treated with a fungicide such as Benomyl or any sulphur-based fungicide.

Clearing out the dead wood from the crown of your tree, removal of affected leaves and a lot of fresh air are other measures that will help restore your tree to health.

False mildew: This fungus is usually found on the undersides of leaves, whence it spreads into the plant. It is recognisable as a grey mouldy coating on the underside with yellow flecks on the top of the leaf. More air should be allowed to get at the plant and it should be sprayed with fungicide.

Azalea gall

where you keep your bonsai take the precaution of spraying it every fourteen days in high summer with 0.2% BASF—Maneb spray powder or any copper-based fungicide. If your pines still produce brown needles in the autumn it won't be a question of pine blight, but simply the annual shedding of old needles.

Azalea gall: The leaves thicken and become misshapen, like 'ear lobes', which are at first covered in a pale green powder, later turning white. Cut off stricken leaves and treat the plant with Zineb or Captan preparations.

Red spot disease: With this disease of maples triggered by a fungal attack, various sized brilliant red pimples appear on the bark. Initially the bark dies back, then the whole branch. The only thing to do in this case is prune back till you reach healthy food.

Pine blight: This is a fungal disease that can attack young pines. In autumn and winter brown spots start to appear on the needles, turning into black diagonal stripes as spring approaches. Before long the entire needle will have died. If blight should attack any trees near

Black spot

Black spot: This is a sooty, black deposit found on leaves, often affecting elm species (*Zelkova*), and usually restricted to one side of the plant. The condition can be treated with Ortho-Phalton 50.

Root rot: This is the commonest disease you will come across and it can have various causes. It can develop because errors have been made in caring for the tree: perhaps it has been over-watered, given too much fertiliser or given the wrong soil mixture. Also, if conditions are too dry, the fine fibrous roots die and later rot when the plant is next watered.

Basically with this disease you must first of all remove all rotted pieces of root; next dip the remaining area of root in a Benomyl or Orthocid solution, and finally repot your tree in new soil. In the early days water sparingly as you must allow time for new fibrous roots to form—until then the plant cannot absorb as much water as a healthy one. Spray your bonsai more often. In addition, keep your tree somewhere shaded and out of the wind.

Obviously you must only begin feeding a plant that has had a damaged root system once enough new roots have formed.

Dying back of twigs: This usually occurs in maples, caused by a fungus. The buds do not open up and the young shoots die back. There is no treatment for this disease, the only solution being to prune back to healthy wood.

Trident maple
Acer buergerianum
broom style
height 40cm
age about 28 years

6 CHINESE BONSAI

Over the centuries the Chinese have developed the same principle for bonsai training as the Japanese. In the first instance they, too, have the desire to learn from nature; both nationalities see bonsai as the art of imitating nature, of creating harmony, of making ourselves aware of that which is essential in life. But there are details of the art which are more important for Chinese bonsai masters than their Japanese counterparts, namely the relationship in size between dish and tree, roots and trunk, trunk and branches.

If you compare bonsai from the two countries one thing you will notice is that the Chinese often choose very large bonsai dishes which are very attractive, very old and precious. Their trees tend to be bigger than the Japanese, too, not infrequently reaching a height of 1m–1.5m and sometimes more. And often, to our Japanese-trained eye, the roots of a Chinese bonsai look very thin in relation to the trunk. These trees simply grow abruptly out of the ground; the trunk is almost the same thickness from top to bottom, scarcely tapering at all as it reaches the crown of the tree.

The relationship in size between trunk and branches is also not so well balanced as in Japanese bonsai. You might find quite thin branches sticking abruptly out of thick trunks, and it is often only in the crown of the tree that you will find any very graceful branches. Sometimes, too, the angle at which branches hang seems to us somewhat audacious.

It is only by looking at Chinese bonsai that we realise how far our minds are ingrained with the Japanese bonsai masters' feel for style. We have become used to their clear, balanced shapes and as yet have not developed a style of our own.

With Japanese bonsai there are most certainly examples where the arrangement has become so much a work of art that it no longer has life; and there are Chinese bonsai where the shape may be cruder, very often making it look odd but giving it a certain naturalness.

In China the following species of plants are the commonest for bonsai training:

Buxus microphylla   small-leaved box
Bougainvillea glabra   lesser bougainvillea
Carmona microphylla   fukien tea
Celtis chinensis   Chinese hackberry
Elaeagnus angustifolia   oleaster
Ficus benjamina   weeping fig
Ficus retusa   fig-tree species
Gardenia jasminoides   gardenia
Glyptostrobus pensilis   Chinese cypress
Jasminum nudiflorum   winter jasmine
Juniperus chinensis   Chinese juniper
Murraya paniculata   jasmine orange
Nandina domestica   sacred bamboo
Pinus parviflora   white pine
Pinus thunbergii   Japanese black pine
Podocarpus macrophyllus   yew podocarpus—Kusamaki
Pseudolarix amabilis   Chinese golden larch
Punica granatum   pomegranate
Sageretia theesans   hedge sageretia
Serissa foetida   serissa (tree of a thousand stars)
Ulmus parviflora   chinese elm

Chinese elm
Ulmus parviflora
height about 74cm
age about 40 years

Orange jasmine
Murraya paniculata, height about 60cm, age about 65 years

Chinese elm
Ulmus parviflora, length about 57cm, age about 95 years

Chinese elm
Ulmus parviflora, height about 55cm, age about 50 years

Sageretia *Sageretia theesans*, in the shape of a dragon,
length about 45cm, age about 55 years

7 INDOOR BONSAI

In Germany where the author lives and works, and in Britain, too, the first attempts at keeping indoor bonsai have only recently been made. But in America bonsai enthusiasts have been wrestling for years with the problem of which species are most suitable for keeping indoors as bonsai, though all plants with small leaves and tree-like branches that are commonly kept as indoor plants can be trained as bonsai.

Most are tropical and subtropical plants and as the temperatures in our living rooms roughly correspond with the native climate of such plants, they are quite at home in them. Small-leaved fig trees, gardenias and waxy-leaved species (*Schefflera* [*Brassaia*] spp.) are particularly suited for indoors. Unlike subtropical, cold-house plants which cannot tolerate room temperatures that are too high, with tropical plants the temperature must not drop below +15°C. Of course, different bonsai styles have to be found for these trees, more in keeping with the shapes found in their native country. Except in the case of fig trees, these new styles often have very little in common with traditional bonsai forms and cannot compete with the fascination and charm of a white pine, for example.

It is with the subtropical, coldhouse plants that you can most closely adhere to the normal bonsai styles. Included here are bougainvilleas, citrus fruits, camellias, myrtles, olives, serissas and others. In winter the most favourable daytime temperatures for these plants lie between about 8° and 12°C, whilst at night they should be a few degrees lower (5–6°C), to correspond with the night and day temperature difference the plants are accustomed to in their homeland. This lower night temperature is particularly important for the plants if they are kept warmer during the day than they actually like, around 12–16°C. You can make the temperature lower for them at night simply by putting the plants in a cooler room. At night directly in front of a window the temperature will in any case be lower than in the rest of the room, and you can reduce it still further by drawing a heavy curtain across to separate off the window area. This creates a kind of cooler climatic zone between the curtain and window. Don't choose a window-sill site for your subtropical plants that is directly above a radiator—that's too much to expect even of tropical plants! In summer these species of bonsai like to be out-of-doors provided they are out of the wind and kept shaded to start with; of course, in autumn when the night temperature drops below +5°C, they should be brought indoors again. If you prefer, they can remain indoors throughout the summer if kept by a window in a cool, bright spot.

With indoor bonsai it is also very important to create conditions that resemble as closely as possible the natural living conditions of the plant. Amounts of light, temperatures and humidity must be right for the plant to be able to flourish.

Because of light requirements the best site for any bonsai is a bright window-sill (as already mentioned, an exception in all this are subtropical plants during summer; a window facing the midday sun would be too hot for them at this time of year.) If such a site is impossible, and the amount of light available is less than favourable, you can give a helping hand with artificial light, for example with a Phillips E 86 (160 watt) bulb switched on for 16 hours during the day in summer and for around 10 hours in winter. To maintain a sufficiently high humidity level it is important for all trees to be sprayed in addition to being watered. The humidity can also be increased by standing your plants together with their pots in large, flat, ceramic dishes filled with a layer of pebblestones or Lytag or Hartag. Excess water from watering and spraying the plants is absorbed by the pebbles and slowly vapourised, thus improving the air circulation at the same time as raising the humidity level immediately surrounding the plants. Liquid fertilisers are most suitable for feeding indoor bonsai, as organic fertilisers, particularly the pellet type, start to smell as they decompose.

A good soil mixture for indoor bonsai consists of humus-rich garden compost mixed with sand, with, in addition, one part loam for older plants; repotting is necessary about once every two years. You can cultivate indoor bonsai from seeds or cuttings or train them from pot plants. At the end of the chapter you will find a list of plants suitable for keeping as indoor bonsai, and in the next few pages you will find detailed descriptions of the most popular species suitable for bonsai training.

SUBTROPICAL PLANTS

Azaleas: *Rhododendron* 'Simpsii'; *R. obtusum*

Native to the Far East: Evergreen shrub with small, shiny, dusky-green leaves; chief flowering period early summer, blossom comes in all colours.

Species with small flowers are particularly suited to bonsai training.

After flowering, the remains of the flowers together with the seed pods should be removed. About four to six weeks later the new shoots will be long enough to be pruned back to one or two leaf pairs.

New shoots growing directly on the trunk and at the root area must be removed immediately.

Any style of tree is possible with *Rhododendron* spp. but their twigs are very brittle so wiring must be carried out very carefully; during the winter months they should not be wired at all.

Siting: During summer either indoors next to a cool, bright window or outdoors in a semi-shaded spot. During winter, a bright window location with a temperature of 6–12°C.

Watering: Plenty of water during the flowering period, otherwise water moderately, but never allow to dry out so much that the soil becomes solid.

Feeding: In summer, with a limefree fertiliser only.

Repotting: Every two years before new shoots appear.

Soil: Peat/sand (70:30) or pure peat with a 10% loam content.

Propagation: Cuttings, grafts.

Camellia *Camellia japonica*

Native to Japan, China: The camellia is an evergreen shrub with a light silver, woody trunk, shiny, dark-green, leathery leaves and beautiful pinky white–red flowers in winter. It grows upright and compactly and is suitable for all bonsai styles.

After blossoming the remains of the flowers should be removed and the old shoots pruned back to two or three leaves. The plant will then produce new leaf and flower shoots which can be wired from late summer to autumn.

Siting: In summer may be placed outside in a lightly shaded spot or kept inside by a cool, bright, easterly window. Keep well ventilated. In winter choose a cool window site with temperatures of 10–12°C.

Watering: Keep moist and use lukewarm water.

Feeding: Apply a peaty organic fertiliser after the flowering period.

Repotting: Every two years before the blossom appears; do not prune roots drastically.

Soil: Acid, pH 4.5–5.5, with moderate humus content. Peat, sand, a little loam (3:2:1).

Propagation: Cuttings, but very difficult.

Camellia in an informal upright style, height about 25cm, age 7 years

Crassula arborescens

Native to South Africa: This tree has many common names, including money tree. It is evergreen with shiny, green, fleshy leaves. This species is very good for bonsai training as its natural growth pattern is like a tree's and needs little improvement—perhaps only a pruning of the shoots and a tidying up of the trunk area. *Crassula* species must not be wired, because the bark of the fleshy branches would be damaged.

Siting: During summer either indoors next to a cool, bright window or outside but shaded from the sun. From early autumn must be kept indoors next to a cool window site, at a temperature of 8–12°C. If too warm, the leaves will drop off.

Watering: Sparingly.

Feeding: Very small amounts of liquid fertiliser and only in summer.

Repotting: Spring every year.

Soil: Equal parts peat, sand.

Propagation: Very easy by means of cuttings.

Jade tree in formal upright style,
height 18cm, age 3 years.
This tree was trained by Henry Lorenz of Oftersheim.

Pomegranate *Punica granatum nana*

Native to the Mediterranean area: A deciduous tree with small, pointed, shiny green leaves, pink-red flowers in summer and early autumn and small apple-like fruits.

After blossoming all the shoots can be pruned back to one or two leaf buds, and again perhaps at the beginning of autumn or the following spring before shoots appear. Deal with any new shoots that subsequently appear as for apricot trees. The pomegranate tree can be trained in any of the upright bonsai styles and may be wired during the summer.

Siting: Either the whole year round indoors at a sunny window where it is well ventilated, or outside during summer in a sunny position; after the leaves have been shed bring inside once more and keep at a cool window site (6–8°C).

Watering: Plenty in summer, very little in winter, but do not allow to dry out.

Feeding: Liquid fertiliser from the appearance of new shoots till the flowering period.

Repotting: Every two years before new shoots appear, in spring.

Soil: An equal parts loam/sand/peat mixture.

Propagation: Cuttings or seeds.

Pomegranate, informal upright style,
height 12cm, age 8 years
Trained by M. Stuy

Myrtle *Myrtus communis*

Native to the Mediterranean area: An evergreen shrub with small, shiny, dark-green leaves and white flowers in early summer. The myrtle can withstand frequent pruning of new shoots and may be wired during the summer. It is easy to train and is suitable for any bonsai style, although the broom shape is probably best.

Siting: Out in the open from early summer in a sun-protected spot or indoors by a cool, well-ventilated window. In winter ideal temperature of 8–12°C; a lower night temperature is very important if the myrtle is kept any warmer than this during the day.

Watering: Plenty in summer, less in winter, but do not allow to dry out.

Feeding: Liquid fertiliser every two weeks after the shoots have appeared till the flowering period. After that once a month throughout the summer.

Repotting: In spring before new shoots appear.

Soil: Peat/loam mixture to which good quantities of sand are added.

Propagation: Cuttings.

Serissa, *Serissa foetida*

Native to China: Also known as 'tree of a thousand stars', Serissa is evergreen with small leaves and white blossom in early summer; the odd flower is possible throughout the year. This species flourishes well and is easy to train by means of pruning after the flowering period and by wiring. After three or four pairs of leaves have formed on the shoots, they can be pruned back to one or two pairs. To maintain a compact appearance, the tree must be pruned back to its old wood every two years. Serissas often react badly to a change of site by shedding much of their foliage, but they recover quickly. When the roots are pruned a penetrating smell is released, the reason why its specific name is *foetida*, Latin for 'stinking'. Serissas are suitable for nearly all styles of bonsai.

Siting: In summer at a very bright window or outside out of direct sunlight. In winter a bright window location with temperatures between 12–16°C.

Watering: Plenty of water in summer, keep evenly moist in winter.

Feeding: Liquid fertiliser from when the first shoots appear to late summer, except during the height of the flowering period.

Repotting: About every two years, in spring, before the shoots appear.

Soil: Equal parts mixture of loam, sand and peat.

Propagation: Very easy by means of cuttings.

Serissa *Serissa foetida*,
exposed root style,
height 25cm,
age about 8 years

Sageretia, *Sageretia theesans*

Native to China: An evergreen shrub with small, shiny, bright green leaves and an interesting, flecked bark, similar to the bark of a plane tree. As yet hardly known in the West although it makes a very good indoor bonsai since in winter, with a sufficiently high humidity level, it can tolerate higher temperatures (18–20°C) without suffering any damage. The new shoots must continually be pruned back to two or three leaf pairs, and any undesirable branches may be removed at any time during the year. May be wired throughout the year except during late spring: all bonsai styles possible. A particularly lovely sageretia is pictured on page 133.

Siting: During summer either a very bright, sunny window location or outside; keep slightly shaded in mid-summer. During winter best kept at a temperature of 12–16°C, although possible at 18–20°C provided the night-time temperature is lowered and the foliage is sprayed additionally throughout the day.

Watering: Plenty of water in summer, less in winter, but keep evenly moist.

Feeding: Liquid fertiliser from the first appearance of shoots throughout the summer. Every two weeks.

Repotting: About every two years before shoots appear.

Soil: Loam/sand/peat mixture (2:1:2).

Propagation: Cuttings.

TROPICAL PLANTS

Australian Umbrella Tree *Schefflera (Brassaia) actinophylla*

Native to Australia: Evergreen shrub with shiny green leaves and long stalks. The trunk remains relatively thin nor does it branch out into a crown like the tropical *Ficus* species.

The schefflera is usually trained as a rock bonsai as it forms mangrove-type roots. Once the trunk has reached the height that suits the rock it should be cut off below the leaves, 'beheaded' as it were. The plant will subsequently produce new shoots. Repeated pruning of this sort makes the plant develop several trunks, keeps it compact and ensures it acquires thicker roots.

Siting: An all-year round window location, as bright as possible—the brighter it is the shorter the leaf stalks and the smaller the leaves. Ideal temperature is 18–22°C, not lower than 15°C. Sch700leras do all right left above a radiator.

Watering: Keep the layer of Lytag or Hortag wet.

Feeding: Once a month add liquid fertiliser when watering or supply with hydroponic fertiliser.

Propagation: Seeds or cuttings.

Fig species, *Ficus benjamina, F. retusa, F. deltoidea* and others

Native to South and South-East Asia: The evergreen, small-leaved fig tree species are particularly good for bonsai training as they produce sturdy trunks, a nicely branching shape and shiny, leathery, small leaves. Any bonsai style is possible. New shoots should repeatedly be pruned back to two or three pairs of leaves; the woody branches and trunk should be wired only loosely, for even after three months the wire may already be cutting into the bark. A nicely branching crown can be achieved as in hardwoods by pruning the leaves in early summer; in addition, the leaves that subsequently grow will be smaller than the ones removed.

Siting: All year round at a bright window location, but not in the full glare of the sun; the brighter the location, the more compact the growth. Avoid sharp changes in temperature and draughts. In winter do not allow the temperature to drop below 18°C.

Watering: In summer during the growing period water profusely, but if kept in a cooler site use somewhat less water; do not keep too moist in winter during the resting period.

Feeding: Liquid fertiliser after the shoots appear to the end of summer.

Repotting: Every two years, in spring.

Soil: Commercially available garden compost that is permeable to water and rich in humus is ideal for fig trees.

Propagation: Seeds and cuttings.

Other popular tropical plants are *Ficus glomerata, F. diversifolia, F. nerifolia, Gardenia jasminoides* and *Polyscias fruticosa*.

Fig tree, broom style,
height 40cm, age 8 years

COLDHOUSE PLANTS

Azalea japonica, A. indica
Buxus microphylla
Bougainvillea glabra
Camellia japonica
Carmona microphylla
Cotoneaster microphyllus
Citrus paradisi, C. reticulata
Cryptomeria japonica
Cupressus arizonica
Cupressus arizonica 'Gold Crest'
Eleagnus multiflora
Fuchsia spp
Hedera helix
Lagerstroemia indica
Myrtus communis
Nandina domestica
Olea europaea
Podocarpus macrophyllus
Punica granatum
Rosmarinus officinalis
Sageretia theesans
Serissa foetida
Ulmus parviflora

Weeping fig *Ficus benjamina*, triple-trunk—Sankan, height about 45cm, age about 15 years

Fig tree *Ficus retusa*, cascade—Kengai, length about 78cm, age about 30 years

Fig tree *Ficus retusa*, informal upright style,
height 35cm, age about 12 years

Fig tree *Ficus retusa*, exposed root—Neagari
height 70cm, age about 100 years.
Here the roots are partially laid bare and adopt the function of the trunk.

172

This old chinese bonsai, a small-leaved weeping fig *Ficus benjamina*, height about 97cm, age about 45 years, is part of the collection belonging to Mr Pin Kewpaisal of Bangkok, Thailand. In a temperate climate this type of bonsai is only suitable for indoors.

Schefflera (Brassaia) actinophylla, growing on lava, age about 4–8 years

A twelve-year-old *Schefflera (Brassaia) actinophylla*, raised from seed, height about 30cm

Fig tree *Ficus deltoidea*, rock-grown—Ishitsuki, height about 48cm, age about 10 years

Bamboo *Bambusa multiplex nana*,
height 25cm, age about 4 years.
This species is suitable as an indoor bonsai.

Appendix 1
IMPORTANT JAPANESE TERMS

Ara-kawacho	Tree with rough bark
Ara-ki	Freshly dug tree, suitable as bonsai material
Bankan	Trunk with many curves—'coiled snake'
Bonkei	Natural landscapes planted in a dish (rocks, plants, animal figures, small houses)
Bunjingi or Bunjin	Bonsai in literati style
Chokkan	Bonsai with upright trunk
Daiki	Parent plant, stock (Tsugi-ho—scion)
Eda-jin	Artificially bleached branches
Eda-nuki	Removal of unwanted branches
Eda-uchi	Harmonising effect of branches
Eda-zashi	Branch pruning
Fukinagashi	Bonsai in windswept style
Gobo-ne	Tap root
Goro-tsuchi	Coarse-grained soil
Ha-gari	Pinching out of leaves
Hamizu	Spraying leaves with water
Hankan	Bonsai with a very coiled trunk
Han-kengai	Bonsai in semi-cascading style
Hariganekake	Wiring a tree
Ha-zashi	Leaf pruning
Hokidachi	Bonsai in broom style
Honbachi	Bonsai dish
Ikadabuke	Bonsai in raft style
Ishitsuki	Rock-grown bonsai
Ju-shin	Top of the tree
Ju-sei	Growth of the tree

Japanese holly *Ilex serrata*, informal upright style—Moyogi, height 48cm, age about 46 years, seen here in its lovely autumnal mantle

Kabudachi	Clump-style bonsai (several trunks from a single root)
Kabuwake	Separation of the root
Kanju	Deciduous trees (hardwoods)
Kannuki-eda	An ugly branch or twig that must be cut off
Kansui	Watering
Karikomi	Pruning of leaves and branches
Kengai	Bonsai in cascading style
Kesho-tsuchi	Decorative soil, silver sand
Keto-tsuchi	Peat
Ko-eda	Very graceful branches
Kokejun	Trunk that tapers towards the top

Komochi	= Sokan; bonsai with twin trunk	Shohaku	Coniferous trees (softwoods)
Kuro-tsuchi	Black loam	Shohin-bonsai	Bonsai no more than 15cm tall
Kuruma-eda	Ugly branch that must be cut off	Shoki	Bonsai reared from collected specimens = Yamadori-shitate (opposite of Misho)
Mame-bonsai	Bonsai less than 10cm tall	Sokan	Twin-trunked bonsai
Meiboku	Old, antique bonsai	Suiban	Shallow dish without a drainage hole
Me-tsumi	Nipping out leaves		
Mi-mono	Fruit-bearing bonsai	Suiseki	Rocky landscape arranged on Suiban
Misho	Raising bonsai from seed		
Misho-mono	Bonsai from seed	Tachia-gari	Trunk region
Mizu-gire	Too dry	Tangei	Bonsai material
Mizu-goke	Sphagnum moss	Tekishin	Removal of shoots
Moyogi	Bonsai in informal upright style	Tocho-shi	A branch that has grown too long
Neagari	Bonsai with exposed roots		
Nebari	Form of the visible roots	Toriki	The technique of obtaining bonsai by air-layering
Nejikan	Bonsai with twisted trunk		
Netsuranari	Bonsai style with several trees growing from a single root.	Toriki-mono	Bonsai obtained through air-layering
Ne-zashi	Root pruning	Tsugi-ho	Scion (Daiki—parent plant)
Oki-goe	Fertiliser in pellet or powder form	Tsugi-ki	The technique of obtaining a bonsai by grafting
Oyaki	Parent tree (with reference to air-layering grafting technique)	Tsugiki-mono	Bonsai obtained from a graft
		Tsuri-o-toru	Securing a plant to a pot or container
Roboku	Old, antique bonsai		
Sabamiki	Bonsai with split trunk	Yamadori	Collecting bonsai from the wild
Saikei	Landscapes with rocks and trees but no figures	Yamadori-shitate	Bonsai collected from the wild
Sankan	Triple-trunked bonsai	Yobi-tsugi	Grafting of a branch
Sashi-ho	Cutting	Yose-ue	Multi-tree or group style, giving appearance of a forest
Sashi-ki	Propagation by means of cuttings		
Seishi	Bonsai training		
Sentei	Tree pruning		
Shakan	Bonsai with a slanting trunk		
Sharimiki	Driftwood style		

Appendix 2
ENGLISH–JAPANESE PLANT NAMES

Apple	Himeringo
Bamboo	Take
Barberry (Berberis)	Shobyaku
Camellia	Tsubaki
Chamaecyparis obtusa	Hinoki
Chinese juniper	Shinpaku
Chinese quince	Karin
Cotoneaster horizontalis	Beni-shitan
Crab-apple	Kaido
Crape myrtle	Hyakujikko
Dogwood *Cornus controversa*	Mizuki
Elm	Akinire
Firethorn (pyracantha)	Tachinbana-modoki
Gardenia	Kuchinashi
Gingko (maidenhair)	Icho
Hondo spruce	Ezo-Matsu
Japanese apricot	Ume
Japanese azalea	Satsuki
Japanese beech	Buna
Japanese black pine	Kuro-Matsu
Japanese cedar	Sugi
Japanese flowering cherry	Fuji-sakura
Japanese, or flowering, quince *Chanomeles cardinalis*	Boke
Japanese holly *Ilex serrata*	Umemodoki
Japanese hornbeam	Soro
Japanese maple	Momiji
Japanese red maple	Deshojo
Japanese red maple 'Dissectum'	Seigen
Japanese spindle tree	Mayumi
Japanese spiraea	Shimotsuke
Japanese white pine	Goyo-Matsu
Japanese wild cherry	Yama-sakura
Japanese witch hazel	Mansaku
Japonica *Chanomeles japonica*	Chojubai
Lilac	Murasaki-hashidoi
Magnolia stellata	Kobushi
Needle juniper	Tosho
Oleaster	Gumi
Pomegranate	Zakuro
Red pine	Aka-Matsu
Small-leaved box tree	Tsuge
Shrubby cinquefoil	Kinrobai
Spindle tree	Mayumi
Stewartia	Natsutsubaki
Thick-barked black pine or Corkbark pine *Pinus thunbergii corticosa*	Nishiki-Matsu
Trident maple	Kaede
Weeping willow	Yanagi
Winter jasmine	Obai
Wisteria floribunda	Fuji
Yew	Ichii
Zelkova = Japanese elm	Keyaki

Appendix 3 **BONSAI STYLES AND SUITABLE** **DISHES KEY TO BONSAI STYLES**			Ishitsuki—clinging-to-rock or rock-grown
	Chokkan—formal upright		Sankan—triple-trunk
	Moyogi—informal upright		Yose-ue—multi-tree or group
	Shakan—slanting		Sokan—twin-trunk
	Fukinagashi—windswept		Kabudachi—clump
	Han-Kengai—semi-cascade		Ikada—raft
	Kengai—cascade		Netsuranari—raft style from roots
	Hokidachi—broom (or besom)		Bunjingi—literati

179

TABLE OF BONSAI DISHES AND APPROPRIATE TREE STYLES

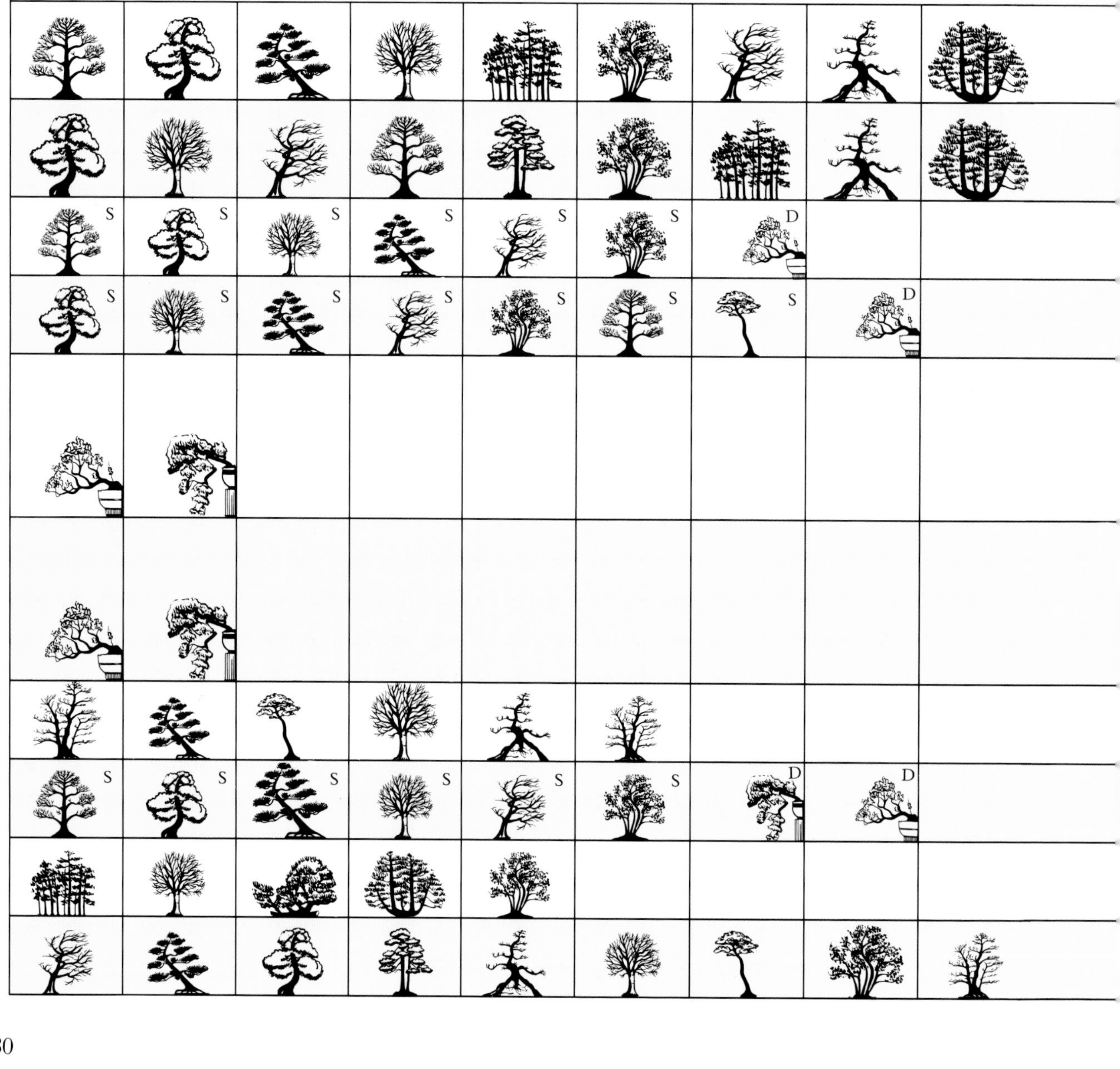

Dish shapes		Position of tree in dish
rectangular dishes		
oval dishes		
square dishes	S D	
round dishes	S D	
tall square dishes		
tall round dishes		
lotus-style dish		
hexagonal or octagonal dishes	S D	
flat slab with or without pedestal		
round flat dish		

S = shallow   D = deep

Appendix 4
BONSAI PLANTS: THEIR CARE AND TRAINING

Hardy means that the plant can tolerate frost. However, as mentioned on page 144, the bonsai should be protected from heavy frost.
Half hardy means that the plant can only withstand a few degrees of frost, up to −5°C, and so should be kept as frost-free as possible over the winter, preferably between 0°C and +8°C.
Tender (non-hardy) means that the plant should be overwintered at a temperature of +4°C to +6°C.

Species	Description	Branch pruning	Pinching out	Wiring
Abies alba European silver fir Pinaceae	evergreen conifer that grows in shape of a pyramid; upright cones	before new shoots appear	Summer, allow new shoots to grow 3cm long then prune them back to 1cm	at all times, except during the growing period
Acer buergerianum Trident maple Aceraceae	deciduous tree with tricorn leaves and brilliant yellow-orange autumnal colouring	before new shoots appear fine branches also in early autumn	summer, pruning back repeatedly to leave 1–3 leaf pairs	after leaf pruning
Acer palmatum Japanese maple Aceraceae	deciduous tree with delicate, green leaves and fine branches. Firy red colour in autumn	before new shoots appear fine branches also in early autumn	after shoots have appeared until early autumn. Reduce back repeatedly to 1–3 leaf pairs	after leaf pruning
Acer palmatum 'Atropurpureum' Aceraceae	deciduous tree with brilliant red new shoots and red autumnal colouring	before new shoots appear fine branches also in early autumn	after shoots have appeared until early autumn. Prune back to 1–3 leaf pairs	after leaf pruning
Amelanchier canadensis June – or Serviceberry Rosaceae	deciduous tree with white flowers, bronze-coloured new shoots and red autumnal colouring	before new shoots appear or after leaves have been shed in autumn	summer, prune shoots back once to 2–3cm long, and shorten any overlong shoots again in early autumn	spring to autumn
Betula nigra River or red birch Betulaceae	very pretty deciduous tree with white trunk, fresh greenery and catkins in spring	before shoots appear	prune new shoots back to 1–2 leaf buds	mid summer
Buxus microphylla Box tree Buxaceae	evergreen, small-leaved bush or tree with yellowy-white bark	before shoots appear	prune new shoots back repeatedly to 2–3 buds	at all times except when very cold
Camellia japonica Camellia Theaceae	evergreen shrub with leathery leaves and white-pink flowers in winter	before shoots appear	after flowering period prune back once to leave 2 buds	mid summer through to early autumn
Carpinus laxiflora Hornbeam Betulaceae	deciduous tree with fine branches, particularly pretty in its spring mantle	before shoots appear	throughout the summer continually prune new shoots back to 1–2 leaf buds	mid summer
Carmona microphylla Fukien tea Rosaceae	evergreen shrub with shiny oval leaves and white flowers in spring and summer	before shoots appear	after the first blossom prune back to 1–2 buds; after the second, reduce to 2 buds	at all times
Cedrus libani Cedar of Lebanon Pinaceae	evergreen coniferous tree with upright cones, makes an impressive sight	before shoots appear	prune new growth in mid summer to leave 2 whorls of needles	at all times

tering   Only general instructions can be given on watering. You will have to find out yourself how much water your plant needs. This
l depend on the temperature, humidity and condition of the plant. Whilst shoots are growing reduce the amount of water somewhat. For
er information turn to page 134.

potting	Siting	Hardiness	Watering	Feeding	pH
fore shoots appear; young nts every 2 years, older es every 5 years	slightly shaded	hardy	plenty	after shoots have appeared until early autumn, plentiful amounts	5.8–6
fore shoots appear; young nts every 1–2 years, older es every 2–3 years	shade slightly in mid-summer	half-hardy	plenty	after shoots have appeared, pellets or liquid fertiliser every 4 weeks	5.5–5.8
fore shoots appear; young nts every 1–2 years, older es every 2–3 years	shade slightly in mid-summer	half-hardy	plenty	after shoots have appeared, pellets or liquid fertiliser every 4 weeks	5.5–5.8
fore shoots appear; young nts every 1–2 years, older es every 2–3 years	shade slightly in mid-summer	half-hardy	plenty	after shoots have appeared, pellets or liquid fertiliser every 4 weeks	5.5–5.8
fore shoots appear; young nts every 2 years, older es every 4–5 years	full sun	hardy	not too much	after shoots have appeared, pellets or liquid fertiliser every 4 weeks	5.8–6.0
fore shoots appear, every 2 ars	full sun	hardy	not too much	every 4 weeks throughout the summer in liquid or pellet form	4.8–5.5
fore shoots appear, every 2 ars	tolerates full sun and shade	half-hardy	plenty	every 4 weeks throughout the summer in liquid or pellet form	5.5–6.0
er flowering period, every years	semi-shade	protect from frost	plenty	in spring and early summer every 14 days, with organic fertiliser	4.4–5.5
fore shoots appear; young es every 2 years, older es every 3–5 years	full sun, airy site	hardy	plenty	after shoots appear until early autumn, every 4 weeks	5.8–6.0
fore shoots appear, every 2 ars	slightly shaded	protect from frost, do not allow temperature to drop below +8°C	plenty	throughout the summer once a month, suspended during the flowering period	5.5–6.0
fore shoots appear; young ants every 2 years, older es every 2–5 years	full sun	half-hardy	plenty	after shoots appear until early autumn, every 4 weeks, pellet fertiliser	5.8–6.0

Species	Description	Branch pruning	Pinching out	Wiring
Celtis chinensis Chinese nettle-tree Ulmaceae	deciduous tree with silvery grey trunk, round crown and oval leaves	before shoots appear	continually prune new growth back to 1–3 buds until early autumn	mid summer
Chaenomeles chinensis False or Chinese quince Rosaceae	deciduous tree with thorny branches, profusely covered with white blossom—pinky red before new shoots appear	spring	after the flowering period prune all shoots back to 1–2 buds, and again in autumn to 4–5 buds	not possible
Chaemaecyparis spp False cypress Cupressaceae	evergreen conifers with scaly leaves; many forms of growth	spring and autumn	nip off new shoots continually to leave 2–3 buds, until autumn	late winter; early autumn
Cotoneaster spp Cotoneaster Rosaceae	evergreen and deciduous forms of this tree. Has various forms of growth. Lovely autumnal colouring with brilliant red berries	spring before shoots appear	prune new shoots back in early summer to leave 2–3 buds; trim long shoots in autumn	at all times
Crassula arborescens Jade tree Crassulaceae	evergreen succulent that grows like a tree, fleshy, dark-green leaves	spring before new shoots appear	prune back new shoots repeatedly to 1–2 leaf pairs	not possible
Crataegus spp Hawthorn Rosaceae	deciduous tree with white, pink or red flowers and red, yellow or black fruits. Lovely autumn colours, very thorny	spring before new shoots appear	in summer reduce new shoots once to 2–3cm, then in autumn trim overlong shoots again	mid-summer
Cupressus sempervirens Italian cypress Cupressaceae	evergreen, fast-growing, pillar-like tree with scaly leaves	spring before new shoots appear	nip off about $\frac{2}{3}$ new shoots continually until the beginning of autumn	late winter, early autumn
Cryptomeria japonica Japanese cedar Taxodiaceae	evergreen, slow-growing conifer, autumnal colouring reddish to dark-brown, a fresh green in spring	early spring	nip off about $\frac{2}{3}$ new shoots continually until the beginning of autumn	early spring, early autumn
Elaegnus angustifolia Oleaster Elaeagnaceae	semi-evergreen bush or tree with thorny branches and narrow, silvery leaves, fruit-bearing	spring before new shoots appear, or early autumn	prune back new shoots to 2–3 buds in early summer	mid-summer
Fagus sylvatica Common or European beech Fagaceae	mighty deciduous tree whose leaves turn brown in autumn and are only shed just before new shoots appear in spring	spring before new shoots appear or early autumn	prune back new shoots in early summer to leave 2–3 buds	mid-summer
Ficus spp Fig tree species Moraceae	evergreen, tropical deciduous tree, the small-leaved species being suitable for bonsai training	at all times	prune back new shoots repeatedly to 2–3 leaves	at all times, but only for 3 months at the most

epotting	Siting	Hardiness	Watering	Feeding	pH
fore shoots appear; young ants every 2 years, older es every 3–4 years	full sun	half-hardy	plenty	after shoots appear until early autumn, every 4 weeks, or use pellet fertiliser	5.5–5.8
ly in early autumn, every years	full sun	hardy	plenty	after flowering period to early autumn, every 14 days	5.8–6.0
ring, every 2 years	slightly shaded	hardy	plenty	throughout the summer every 4 weeks	5.5–5.8
fore new shoots appear; ung plants every 1–2 years, der ones every 2–4 years	full sun	hardy	plenty	after new shoots appear until early autumn, every 14 days	5.5–5.8
fore new shoots appear in ring, every 2 years	semi-shaded	not below +5°C	very sparingly	mid-summer, once a month	5.5–5.8
fore new shoots appear in ring; young plants every 2 years, older ones every 5 years	full sun	hardy	plenty	after new shoots appear until late summer, once a month	5.8–6.0
ring, every 2 years	full sun	protect from frost	plenty	throughout the summer every 4 weeks	5.5–5.8
ring, every 2 years	full sun	half-hardy	plenty	every 4 weeks throughout the summer	5.5–5.8
fore new shoots appear; ung plants every 1–2 years, der ones every 3–5 years	full sun	hardy	not too much	after new shoots appear to the beginning of autumn every 14 days	5.8–6.0
fore new shoots appear; ung plants every 1–2 years, der ones every 3–5 years	full sun	hardy	plenty	after new shoots appear until the beginning of autumn, every 4 weeks	5.8–6.0
spring, every 2 years	indoors not below 18°C	protect from frost	not too much	spring and mid-summer every 4 weeks	5.5–6.0

Species	Description	Branch pruning	Pinching out	Wiring
Gardenia jasminoides Gardenia Rubiaceae	evergreen, thickly branched shrub with shiny, oval leaves and highly perfumed, white flowers	spring before new shoots appear	after the flowering period prune all shoots back to 2–3 leaf pairs, in summer prune new growth again to 2–3 buds	mid-summer
Ginkgo biloba Maidenhair tree Ginkgoaceae	the oldest tree of our planet, has existed for 200 million years. Deciduous with long-stalked, fan-like leaves and golden autumnal colouring	spring before new shoots appear	in young plants prune new shoots back to 4–5 leaves, 1–2 in older ones	mid-summer
Hedera helix Ivy Araliaceae	evergreen climbing plants with different shaped leaves, greenish-yellow flowers and black, berry-like fruits	spring	continually prune new shoots back to 2–3 leaves	at all times
Jasminum nudiflorum Winter jasmine Oleaceae	deciduous, robust shrub with four-cornered, overhanging branches and yellow flowers in winter	spring	after flowering prune back all shoots to 1–2 buds, reduce new shoots in mid summer to 2–3 buds	mid-summer
Juniperus chinensis Chinese juniper Cupressaceae	genus containing 45 species ranging from very far north to the Mediterranean region	spring, beginning of autumn	nip off new shoots by $\frac{2}{3}$ continually until the beginning of autumn	early spring, early autumn
Juniperus rigida Needle or temple juniper Cupressaceae	evergreen conifer with sharp needles in whorls of 3, and fleshy blue, green and reddish cones	early spring	continually nip off new shoots to leave 0.5cm, until beginning of autumn	early spring, early autumn
Larix decidua European larch Pinaceae	deciduous conifer, fast-growing in juvenile period; needles turn a golden colour in autumn and subsequently drop off. Needles grouped in bunches, upright cones.	spring before new shoots appear	prune back new shoots through the summer to leave 2 whorls of needles	early spring, early autumn
Magnolia spp Magnolia Magnoliaceae	most magnolias are deciduous trees, often flowering before new shoots appear. Flowers range from star to tulip shaped, in white	spring before new shoots appear	after flowering prune shoots back to 2 buds	mid-summer
Malus halliana Crab apple Rosaceae	charming deciduous tree with shiny, oval leaves, deep pink flowers at the end of purple stalks and red apples the size of cherries in autumn–winter	spring before new shoots appear	prune back new shoots in mid-summer to 1–2cm, trim long shoots in early autumn back to 1cm	mid-summer
Picea spp Spruce Pinaceae	robust, evergreen conifers with pyramidal growth and hanging cones	early spring, autumn	allow new shoots to grow to 2cm long until mid-summer then trim back to 0.5–1cm	autumn and winter

Repotting	Siting	Hardiness	Watering	Feeding	pH
...efore new shoots appear, in ...ring, every 2 years	semi-shaded or indoors	protect from frost	plenty	all summer to the beginning of autumn, every 4 weeks	5.5–6.0
...efore new shoots appear in ...ring; young plants every ...–2 years, older ones every ...–5 years	full sun	hardy	plenty	throughout spring and summer, every 4 weeks	5.8–6.0
...efore new shoots appear in ...ring; young plants every ...–2 years, older ones every ...–5 years	full sun and semi-shade or indoors	hardy	plenty	throughout spring and summer, every 14 days	5.8–6.0
...ter flowering in spring, or ...rly autumn, every 2 years	full sun	hardy	plenty	every 6 weeks from early spring through to autumn	5.8–6.0
...efore new shoots appear, ...very 2 years	full sun	hardy	plenty	every 4 weeks from spring to autumn	5.8–6.0
...efore new shoots appear, ...very 2 years	full sun	hardy	plenty	every 4 weeks from spring to autumn	5.8–6.0
...efore new shoots appear, ...very 2 years	full sun	hardy	plenty	every 4 weeks from spring to autumn	5.5–5.8
...efore shoots appear, every 2 ...ears	full sun	hardy	not too much	after flowering until early autumn, every 4 weeks	5.8–6.0
...nnually in early autumn	full sun	hardy	plenty	after flowering until early autumn, every 4 weeks	5.5–6.5
...efore new shoots appear or ...n early autumn, every 2 years	full sun, slightly shaded in mid-summer	hardy	plenty	every 4 weeks throughout late spring and summer and into autumn	5.5–5.8

Species	Description	Branch pruning	Pinching out	Wiring
Pinus spp Pine (2-needled) Pinaceae	fast-growing, evergreen conifers with anything from short to long needles and small, hanging cones	early spring, autumn	completely remove new shoots in mid-summer (*see* p. 84)	autumn and wint
Pinus parviflora 'Pentaphylla' Japanese white pine Pinaceae	slow-growing, five-needled pines with small needles steel-blue-green in colour	early spring, autumn	prune candles by $\frac{1}{3}-\frac{2}{3}$ before they unfold in early summer	autumn and wint
Podocarpus macrophylla Podocarpus—Kusamaki Podocarpaceae	evergreen trees and shrubs with needles arranged in spirals	before new shoots appear, spring	when new shoots have reached a length of about 3cm in early summer prune back to 1cm	spring, early autu
Potentilla fruticosa Rosaceae	deciduous shrub with interesting, red-brown bark and bright green, gently toothed leaves, yellow flowers from early summer to autumn	before new shoots appear in spring	only prune back last year's shoots to 1–2 buds before new shoots appear	mid-summer
Prunus mume Japanese apricot Rosaceae	deciduous tree with white-pink flowers in mid winter	after flowering period in early spring	prune back all shoots after the flowering period to 2–3 buds; trim the tips of all shoots in late summer and prune again in early autumn to 4–5 buds	mid-summer
Prunus serrulata Japanese cherry Rosaceae	wild cherry from the Far East, a deciduous tree with upright branches and brown bark; white-pink flowers in late spring	after flowering period in spring	after flowering prune back all shoots to 2 buds, then take back new growth to 2–3 buds	mid-summer
Pyracantha angustifolia Fire-thorn Rosaceae	evergreen, thorny deciduous tree with white flowers in summer and rich red and yellow fruits in autumn and early winter	before new shoots appear, in spring	prune back new shoots in spring to 2 buds and trim overlong shoots in early autumn	mid summer
Serissa foetida Serissa Rubiaceae	delicate, evergreen deciduous tree with narrow, oval, opposed leaves and small, white flowers	at all times	after blossoming prune back all shoots to 1–2 leaf pairs	at all times
Taxus cuspidata Japanese yew Taxaceae	evergreen conifers with broad dark-green needles and fire-red, fleshy seeds	before new shoots appear in spring	when new shoots have grown about 3cm long (early summer) prune back to 1cm	early spring, autu
Zelkova serrata Japanese or grey-barked elm Ulmaceae	deciduous trees with upright trunk, long, splayed branches and small, oval, toothed leaves	before new shoots appear in spring	prune back new shoots continually until early summer to 1–3 buds	mid-summer

epotting	Siting	Hardiness	Watering	Feeding	pH
efore new shoots appear or rly autumn, every 2–3 ears	full sun	hardy	plenty	every 4 weeks throughout late spring, summer and into autumn	5.8–6.0
efore new shoots appear or early autumn, every 2–3 ears	full sun	hardy	not too much	every 4 weeks throughout late spring, summer and into autumn	5.8–6.0
efore new shoots appear, very 1–2 years	full sun to semi-shaded	protect from frost	plenty	twice in early summer, twice in early autumn	5.8–6.0
efore new shoots appear, very 1–2 years	full sun	hardy	plenty	once per month throughout spring and summer	5.5–5.8
ter the flowering period, very 1–2 years	full sun	half-hardy	not too much	every 4 weeks from spring through to mid-summer	5.8–6.0
ter flowering period, every –2 years	full sun	hardy	not too much	after flowering, every 4 weeks from late spring to the beginning of autumn	5.8–6.0
efore new shoots appear, in ring every 2 years	full sun	hardy	plenty	from late spring to the beginning of autumn, every 4 weeks, except during blossoming period	5.5–5.8
efore new shoots appear, very 1–2 years	slightly shaded	protect from frost	plenty	once per month from spring throughout the summer	5.5–5.8
efore new shoots appear, very 1–2 years	full sun to semi-shaded	hardy	not too much	twice in early summer and twice in early autumn at monthly intervals	5.8–6.0
efore new shoots appear; oung plants every 2 years, lder ones every 3–4 years	full sun	half-hardy	plenty	after flowering to early autumn, every 4 weeks, or pellet fertiliser	5.5–5.8

Appendix 5
SOME GOOD BONSAI SUBJECTS:
THEIR SHAPES AND LEAVES

The leaf outlines will help you identify plants you have collected whilst the tree shapes may provide some ideas for bonsai training.

Larix europaea (or decidua)
European larch

Sagaretia theesans
Sagaretia

Fagus crenata
Japanese white beech

Cedrus deodara
Deodar or Himalayan cedar

Zelkova serrata
Japanese zelkova
or grey-barked elm

Taxus baccata
Common yew

Ginkgo biloba
Maidenhair tree

Tsuga canadensis
Eastern or Canadian hemlock

Cedrus atlantica
Atlas cedar

Cedrus libani
Cedar of Lebanon

Ulmus carpinifolia
Smooth-leaved elm

Acer pseudoplatanus
Sycamore

Picea abies
Norway spruce

Pinus silvestris
Scots pine

Quercus robur
English or pedunculate oak

Salix babylonica
Weeping willow

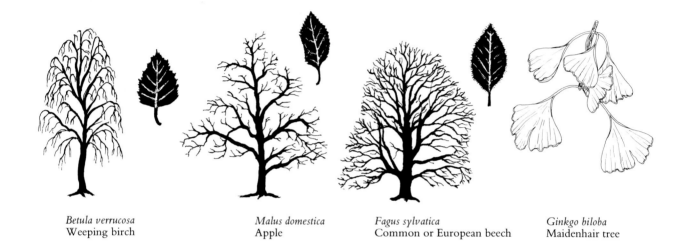

Betula verrucosa
Weeping birch

Malus domestica
Apple

Fagus sylvatica
Common or European beech

Ginkgo biloba
Maidenhair tree

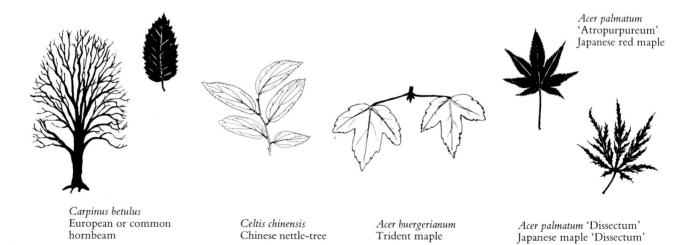

Acer palmatum
'Atropurpureum'
Japanese red maple

Carpinus betulus
European or common
hornbeam

Celtis chinensis
Chinese nettle-tree

Acer buergerianum
Trident maple

Acer palmatum 'Dissectum'
Japanese maple 'Dissectum'

Appendix 6
SEASONAL CULTURAL GUIDE

MID WINTER

Siting
Bonsai need to be overwintered in a bright spot, but if the sunlight is strong they must be shaded, for the warmth may start to rouse a tree from its winter sleep. The winter sun may be sufficiently powerful to warm up the finer branches of a tree without being strong enough to thaw out the root ball, so that the sap begins to flow only in the branches. Water is then evaporated at a pace the roots cannot keep up with and the branches sustain burning damage.

Also check that your bonsai will not be in danger from snow falls should the site be under the eaves of a roof or beneath large trees in the garden.

Watering
Check frequently that your bonsai are moist enough. Trees kept outside over winter should not be sprayed, but watered moderately.

Feeding
No fertiliser during the resting period.

Pests and Diseases
All bonsai can tolerate a winter spray to prevent attack by pests and fungal diseases, but it must be carried out before new shoots appear. As the season progresses move towards the early spring programme.

EARLY SPRING

Siting
If there is no frost around, uncover your bonsai in their winter quarters, but cover them up again if there is any danger of frost.

Watering
Many bonsai start producing new shoots around this time and so will need more water. It is watering that determines growth, so don't water too profusely otherwise the shoots will develop much more quickly, the gaps between the leaves will be that much greater and the leaves themselves bigger.

Feeding
After the first shoots have appeared begin applying fertiliser, but sparingly, otherwise the shoots will get too thick.

Repotting
Nearly all types of bonsai can be repotted before the first shoots appear until the first leaves develop. Don't forget to prune the roots. Since conifers produce shoots later, they can be repotted up until the beginning of summer.

Pests and Diseases
You should now undertake a spring programme of spraying bonsai to protect them from harmful insects and fungal diseases.

Branch Pruning
All unwanted branches can now be removed before shoots start to appear, and wiring can be started (see Table, p. 182).

It depends on where you live, but early spring is usually a suitable time for collecting bonsai from the wild. Once the ground has thawed out and the plants have come to life again, trees can be dug out easily and transplanted. High up in the mountains this won't be possible until early summer.

Early spring is the time for sowing seeds and carrying out grafts before shoots start to appear; it is also the right time for taking conifer cuttings.

EARLY SUMMER

Siting
Transfer your bonsai to their summer locations but still keep them protected from frost. Most bonsai like a sunny site, with only very sensitive hardwoods, such as maples, needing to be shielded from very strong sunlight, (see Table, p. 182). From time to time remember to turn your trees to allow them to develop equally on all sides.

Watering
In warmer weather plants need more water but be careful not to soak them. In fact, pines, which are developing candles at this time, produce much shorter needles if watered sparingly. If very hot, trees should be sprayed only in the mornings and in late afternoon.

Feeding
The faster-growing deciduous trees need more fertiliser than the slower-growing conifers. Alternate your fertilisers, perhaps using an organic one first, then a liquid one.

Repotting
Trees, such as conifers, that produce shoots late and some deciduous trees may still be repotted at this time.

Pruning
In late spring and early summer the new shoots on all types of bonsai should be pruned back, and removed completely on black pines. Leaf pruning on deciduous trees is possible up until mid summer, and many of them can be wired until then.

Deciduous tree cuttings may be taken until early summer.

MID SUMMER

Siting
If necessary keep your bonsai shaded and continue to turn them now and again.

Watering

As in early summer spray only early in the morning and late in the afternoon; otherwise water only into the dishes. In hot summers it is a good idea to cover the earth completely with moss to reduce evaporation and protect the roots from the heat. If kept well watered, prevented from drying out with damp moss, and also kept in the shade, your bonsai should be able to last two or three days without water even in summer.

Feeding

If very hot, stop giving fertiliser. In general feed less during this period as the main growing period is over.

Pruning

With many plants shoot pruning is still necessary.

Heel and other grafts can be carried out on conifers at this time.

EARLY AUTUMN

Siting

Frost-sensitive species may already have to be protected from night frost.

Watering

Depending on atmospheric conditions, more or less watering may be necessary.

Feeding

The last feed may be given at the beginning of this period. To encourage the maturation of the wood and to increase the general resistance of the tree patent potash or potassium sulphate may be given in addition.

Repotting

Non-sensitive species like pines may be repotted now.

Conifers may be wired at this time.

Pests and Diseases

It may be necessary to spray deciduous trees against mildew. This fungus often forms when trees are sprayed too late and are unable to dry off sufficiently before the evening descends.

Seeds may be gathered at this time and cuttings taken from conifers. As autumn sets in remove old needles and superfluous branches from pine trees, and with flowering species such as apricot trees, trim back the shoots to leave four or five flower buds.

EARLY WINTER

Siting

Transfer your trees to their winter quarters.

Watering

Water your bonsai thoroughly before taking them to their winter quarters and then make sure the earth is always kept slightly moist.

Grafts may be performed on conifers throughout the winter months.